THE INSTRUMENTS OF

TORTURE

W9-CEK-338

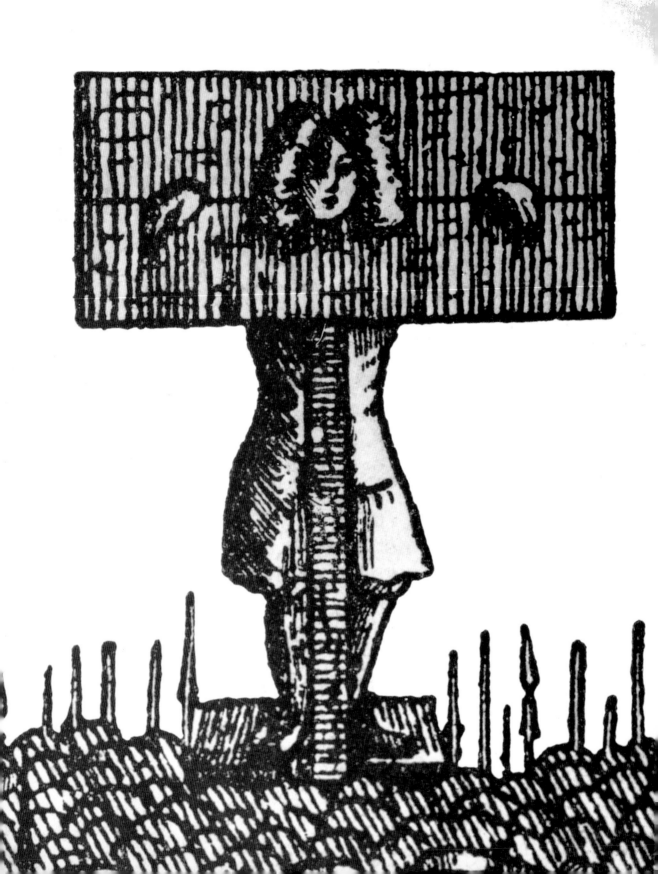

THE INSTRUMENTS OF
TORTURE

Michael Kerrigan

The Lyons Press

This edition first published 2001 by the Lyons Press

Printed in Italy - Nuova GEP, Cremona

Editorial and design by:
Amber Books Ltd
Bradley's Close
74–77 White Lion Street
London N1 9PF

Project Editor: Jill Fornary
Design: Floyd Sayers
Picture Research: Lisa Wren

10 9 8 7 6 5 4 3 2 1

Library of Congress Cataloguing-in-Publication Data held on file

ISBN 1-58574-247-3

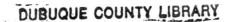

Contents

Brandenburgische halßgerichts

ordnung

Introduction

In 1991, in the days following the bloody conclusion to the pro-democracy demonstrations in Beijing's Tiananmen Square, the Chinese secret police swept the country to pick up those considered subversives and political enemies. One was Zhu Xiaodan, a radical intellectual, whose views alone were held to be crimes against the state. Whisking him away to a detention centre, his captors went to work on both his body and his mind:

> Every day I would wake up, and at a set time would be taken to the interrogation room. They would just repeat over and over again 'confess, confess'. They beat me as well. Sometimes other people came into the room; they would tie me to the bed and beat me with sticks ... Sometimes they would bend me forwards, and tie my arms to my feet, which were attached to the chair. They kept me like that for a whole day, without any food or drink, or going to the toilet. All the time I was being bitten by mosquitoes. I couldn't stand it. In that period, my mind almost broke, exploded.

It may have been no consolation to Zhu Xiaodan to reflect that others like him have suffered likewise down the ages. Nor is he likely to have drawn comfort from the thought that his torture was illegal, having been outlawed by a UN Convention in 1984. The Convention defined torture as:

> Any act by which severe pain or suffering, whether physical or mental, is intentionally inflicted on a person for such purposes as obtaining from him or a third person information or a confession, punishing him for an act he or a third person has committed, or intimidating or coercing him or a third person for any reason based on discrimination of any kind, when such pain or suffering is inflicted by or at the instigation of or with the consent or acquiescence of a public official or other person acting in an official capacity.

'Officially', of course, nothing happened to Zhu Xiaodan. Of the 123 countries estimated by the Torture Survivors' Network to be employing torture, few, if any, would be prepared to acknowledge the fact. A regime

A world of horror is set forth in Erhard Schoen's pictorial inventory of the resources at the disposal of the torturers of Nuremberg, Germany, in the early 16th century, the various instruments being arrayed among rivers of blood.

Two prisoners are flayed, while two more have been beheaded, demonstrating the inadvisability of resisting Assyrian rule. The ancient Assyrians were early masters of the art of torture as a tool of propaganda, as this carved wall relief, circa 750 BC, graphically shows.

that feels no accountability to its own subjects or a conquered people is hardly likely to refrain from such a thoroughly tried and tested method of establishing authority and maintaining control. The Assyrians had worked this out three and a half thousand years ago – there was no better way of quelling unrest in a newly invaded nation than flaying its leaders alive or pegging them out in the sun to dry on the city walls. There is little reason to believe that modern civilizations think any differently. Not only is torture effective in imposing order, but its proponents argue that in the long run it saves lives, by putting down resistance. 'Suppose', asks American philosopher Michael Levin, 'a terrorist has hidden an atomic bomb on Manhattan Island which will detonate at noon on 4 July. Suppose further, that he is caught at 10 a.m. that fateful day, but – preferring death to failure won't disclose where the bomb is … If the only way to save those lives is to subject the terrorist to the most excruciating possible pain, what grounds can there be for not doing so?'

Versions of Levin's argument have been offered for many centuries by those determined to 'protect' their fellow citizens from everything from foreign domination and political subversion to religious heresy and witchcraft. In England, for instance, the use of torture was never recognized in a legal tradition that upheld the presumption of innocence and trial by jury. Yet kings and queens of the Reformation felt justified in using it freely against the threat of religious upheaval. While the immediate purpose of such torture was to elicit information (whether the confession of personal guilt or the identities and whereabouts of confederates), it served the additional purpose of intimidating the wider population. Many would suggest that creating a general atmosphere of terror is, in practice, the true value of torture for the repressive state.

Torture and Truth

'How may I torture him?' asks the judge in Aristophanes' comedy *The Frogs* (circa 406 BC). The reply comes back:

> Why anything!/
> The rack, the wheel, the whip ... skin him alive ... /
> Vinegar up his nose ... bricks on his chest ... /
> Or hang him up by his thumbs ... what have you ... /

While historians are unsure precisely what was meant by 'the wheel' here, the rest of these tortures are all too readily recognizable. The ancient attitude to torture as a means of extracting information was, however, rather more complicated. The ancient Greek word for torture was 'basanos', a name that derived from a touchstone used to test the purity of gold. Basanos was a type of dark, flinty slate, which when rubbed with gold of sufficient quality retained a peculiar mark that no baser alloy could reproduce. What basanos was to the classical banker, torture would become to the ancient judge: the only really reliable method of establishing whether a witness was telling the truth.

Freeborn citizens were never tortured in ancient Greece – it was believed that their 'noble' natures prevented them ever voicing a falsehood. But when slaves were interrogated, torture was not only permissible, but mandatory. No testimony from a slave could be admitted in an Athenian court if it had not been thoroughly tested by the touchstone of torture. The belief that extreme pain was the guarantee of truth seems crazily counterintuitive to us today. Our instincts tell us that a tortured witness will agree to absolutely anything. But our view is rooted in a very modern philosophical sense of the

Many would suggest that creating an atmosphere of terror is the true value of torture

individual self as an autonomous being in possession of its own truth. To the Greeks and Romans the truth was something impersonal, separate from, and greater than, any individual – certainly anyone of low status or captive birth.

A comparable view was found in the Europe of the 15th and 16th centuries. Truth was held to reside not in the witness's words, but in his living flesh. Profoundly sceptical of the value of verbal testimony, a legal manual of the time counselled close attention to what we would now call body language:

> The judge must have his eyes fixed upon the accused, during the whole time that he interrogates him, and must observe all his movements with attention. If the accused trembles, if he weeps, or sighs, the judge will ask him the cause of these movements. Also, if he falters, or if he hesitates; if he is slow, and considers his responses; the judge will press him with reiterated questions …

The truth was thought to be locked up in the living body of the witness: the torturer's task was to prise it out through the medium of pain. Such a view seems less strange when we consider the evidence of Sheila Cassidy, an English surgeon arrested and tortured in Pinochet's Chile in 1975. Stripped naked, to bring home to her the vulnerability of her body, she was stretched out and tied down on an iron bedstead wired up to an electrical current. While one electrode was pushed deep into her vagina, another, 'a wandering pincer', ranged over her body to throw her flesh into spasm wherever her persecutors chose. Under such an assault, she says, 'I found it quite impossible to lie for the shocks came with such frequency and intensity that I could no longer think.' Even if she had wanted to lie, the pain prevented her from doing so.

At the level of individual subjectivity, then, the classical theory would to some extent still seem to hold true. By and large, though, the modern era has seen the philosophical correspondence between body and truth being progressively weakened. In the 17th century, Descartes' famous duality of physical body and spiritual soul ratified what, from then on, would be the strict separation of these two realms. Torture continued, of course, but its rationale was now that the body's pain was the physical lever that could be leaned upon to force an individual to utter truths held privately in the mind. The truth was no longer perceived as an impersonal thing residing in the individual's body.

The process of extracting the truth by torture had once appeared to possess an all but sacramental quality; now it was seen as the brutal

'I found it quite impossible to lie for the shocks came with such frequency and intensity ...'

As yet unbanished to its own separate, secret 'chambers', torture was considered a respectable part of the legal process well into the early modern period, as this 15th-century woodcut clearly shows.

means to a particular end – a necessary evil, perhaps, but an evil nevertheless. From the Enlightenment of the 18th century onwards we start to see moves towards the abolition of torture.

As early as the 16th century the French thinker Montaigne had registered his distaste for what he regarded as nothing less than state-sponsored sadism:

> I could hardly persuade myself, before I saw it with my eyes, that there could be found out souls so cruel, who for the sole pleasure of murder would commit it; would hack, and lop off the limbs of others; sharpen their wits to invent unusual torments, and new kinds of deaths, without hatred, without profit, and for no other end, but only to enjoy the pleasant spectacle of the gestures and motions, the lamentable groans and cries of a man in anguish. For this is the utmost point to which cruelty can arrive.

His protest was increasingly taken up in the century that followed, and by the 18th century writers such as Voltaire were speaking out scathingly against the barbarity of torture. In 1708, Scotland abolished torture, followed in 1740 by the Prussia of Frederick the Great – a tough

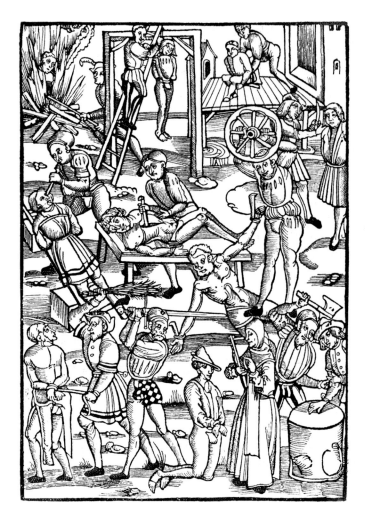

This bloodfest is exaggerated, but the picture it presents of early 16th-century Germany still contains some truth. The religious conflicts of this period created a climate of paranoia in which extremes of cruelty were considered justified.

military monarch. The case against torture was being made clamorously now, with Italian writer Cesare Bonesa Beccaria delivering what many regarded as the clinching argument in his eloquent 'Essay on Crimes and Punishments' (1764):

No man can be judged a criminal until he be found guilty … If guilty, he should only suffer the punishment ordained by the laws, and torture becomes useless, as his confession is unnecessary. If he be not guilty, you torture the innocent; for in the eyes of the law, every man is not guilty, whose crimes have not been proved.

Denmark discontinued torture in 1771. Spain outlawed the practice in 1790, France in 1798 and Russia in 1801. These developments must of course be regarded with some scepticism, since actual practice was not necessarily a genuine reflection of official policy. Nevertheless, they remain significant in revealing how attitudes were shifting: having been an avowed instrument of state, torture was on its way to becoming its guilty secret. The Enlightenment does genuinely seem to have lived up to its name, at least to the extent that torture receded from the official foreground to the secret back rooms of state control.

For most of Europe, most of the time, widespread torture became a thing of the past. Not that there was any shortage of exceptions to this general rule – in Tsarist Russia, for instance, or under the ruthless rule of Lenin or Stalin, not to mention Hitler's Nazis and the Fascists in wartime Europe, as well as those kindred spirits who ruled afterwards in Greece, Portugal and Spain. The consensus was, however, that these were pariah regimes: Torture, it was widely held, had no part to play in respectable government.

Such views did not seem to apply in Europe's overseas colonies, where the indigenous peoples were often feared and despised as savages, and discipline was imposed through physical pain. Colonial conditions gave a *carte blanche* to European sadists. Raoul de Premorel, an agent supervising rubber production along the Kasai river in King Leopold's Belgian Congo, enjoyed dosing perceived malingerers with large quantities of castor oil. When native workers, desperately attempting to meet their weight quota, added dirt or pebbles to their rubber, another agent, Alberic Detiäge, made them eat it. Englishman Sir Francis Galton, one of the founders of late 19th-century race theory, recommended the application of boiling water or hot sand to the naked bodies of recalcitrant porters. In the plantations of the Americas, meanwhile, black slaves were suffering terrible abuses. Long after torture had been rejected in Europe, its use was accepted without question by Europeans overseas.

Torture and technology

'The basic tools of the torturer are his fists and boots', writes one modern commentator. 'Nothing else is really needed to inflict suffering.' And it is true to say that in a thousand army barracks and police stations the world over, much agonizing pain and many hideous injuries have been inflicted by bullying roughs armed with nothing more elaborate than that. Alternatively, perpetrators may equip themselves simply with whatever comes to hand – a knife, a belt, a bottle or a burning cigarette.

When most of us think of torture, however, we tend to think of something more hi-tech: a chamber packed with strange machinery, all wheels and ratchets and sinister-looking hooks. This is not simply a matter of us having seen too many horror films. Down the centuries, regimes and institutions have developed means of torture far more sophisticated and systematic than a simple beating.

This mystification of brutality has profound implications. It allows torturers to believe they are acting not out of base cruelty, but disinterested propriety. The idea of impersonality is central to this particular vision. The Spanish Inquisition and the Soviet KGB, for example, employed torture for what they considered the loftiest of motives. Both kept meticulous records that lent an air of clerical correctness to acts of sheer savagery. Thus the appeal of what were in their day such advanced technologies as the rack and thumbscrews.

Like the Soviet 'psychiatrists' who, equating dissident views with mental instability, dosed their 'patients' with state-of-the-science, mind-tormenting drugs, the priests who served the Inquisition believed they

'The basic tools of the torturer are his fist and boots. Nothing else is needed to inflict suffering'

were not motivated by personal rancour, but simply acting for the general good – of God, His Church, Catholic society and even their victims. Hence the hooded anonymity of the torturer, and the quiet-spoken, scholarly manner of the inquisitor himself. Hence, too, conversely, the gravity of the breakdown in decorum recorded by the Franciscan Friar Angelo Clareno in Italy in around 1304, when one inquisitor found himself driven beyond endurance by the pious stoicism of one particular set of victims:

> That inquisitor, although he was a learned man and of noble family, was so demented by fury that he began to inflict torture with his own hands. When one of the brothers who was to be tortured devoutly recommended himself to Christ, he was so insane with anger that he struck the man on the head and neck. He hit the man so hard that he drove him to the ground like a ball.

It was essential to the mystique of the proceedings that the inquisitor should not commit the torture with his own hands, and should certainly not allow ill-temper to sully what had been held up to all as the transcendent workings of divine justice.

Theatre of pain

If, by descending to the level of the squad-room thug, the representative of the Holy Office was seen to be debasing what should have been a sacred rite, his outburst also contradicts the premise of torture as a ritual process in which anticipation and suspense are deployed as precisely as pain. Torture has always been theatrical to some extent, with the scope to dramatise the most diabolical fantasies of the torturer as well as his victim's darkest nightmares. Examples such as the interminable, exruciatingly regular drip, drip, drip of the 'Chinese water torture', and Poe's pendulum – swinging closer and closer by infinitesimal, terrifying degrees – are probably myths; yet, however fanciful, they are not without some foundation in real fact. Fear and anxiety may be as potent as pain in overwhelming resistance. The first step in the Inquisition's torture was simply to show the victim the instruments of torture and explain their applications. For many heretics, this was quite enough to secure a recantation.

In 1989, the American nun Sister Diana Ortiz was seized by security agents in Guatemala. She later told a Washington congressional committee that she was 'lowered into a pit where injured women, children and men writhed and moaned, and the dead decayed, under

It was essential to the proceedings that the inquisitor should not commit the torture with his own hands

During the decades of the Cold War, the KGB Headquarters in Moscow's Dzerzhinsky Square came to occupy much the same place in the popular imagination as the dungeons of the Inquisition had assumed in an earlier age.

swarms of rats'. Such a scene is a waking nightmare, almost artistically contrived, its impact residing more in its power to unsettle and unhinge than in any physical pain involved (though there had been any amount of that in Sister Ortiz's earlier torture). The Kurdish village elder forced to eat manure by Turkish troops may not be enduring pain as such, but, in being forced to conquer all his normal reflexes and feelings, he is as assuredly being tortured as his younger kin who are beaten or electrocuted. When Belgian soldiers in the Congo forced teenage boys to rape their mothers, the shock for both could hardly have been quantified in physical terms. Torturers have known for many centuries that being coerced into violating one's most powerful taboos is almost as hard to bear as physical violation.

At its most sophisticated, torture engages as much with the mind and imagination as with the body, and the torturer who manages to divine and realize his victim's secret fears has the most effective possible tool for ensuring his or her cooperation. The accomplished torturer can sense and exploit his intimate, if one-sided, relationship with his victim, and can orchestrate the sufferer's periods of agony and respite in order to tease out the drama into a carefully crafted narrative – of pain inflicted, and information surrendered.

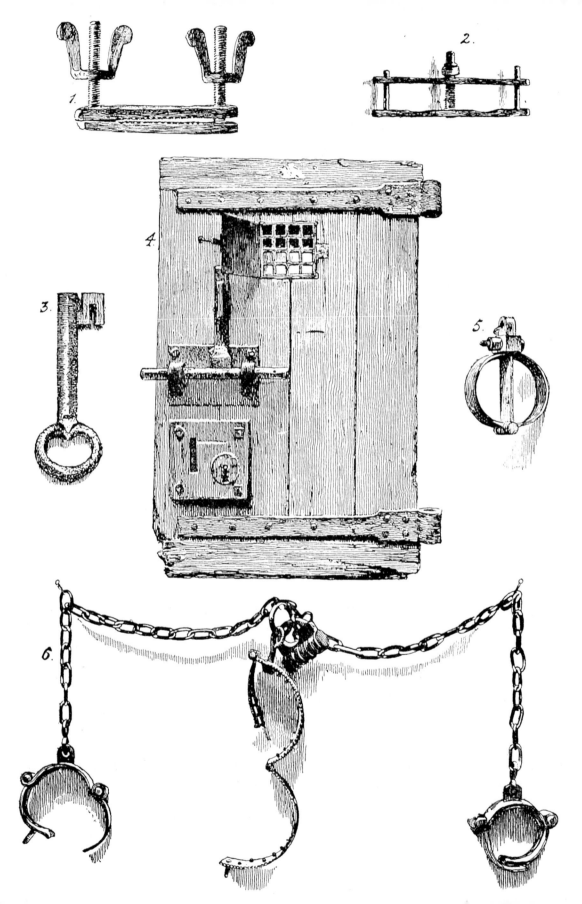

Chapter One

Under Lock and Key

Most people would agree that the deprivation of liberty is a torment in itself, though it might not necessarily be described as a 'torture'. But at what point does mere 'imprisonment' cease, and 'torture by confinement' begin? In testimony given to the human rights organization Amnesty International, Somali businessman Osman Gedi Guled, a prisoner of the Saudi authorities in the 1990s, makes no claim to have been beaten or electrocuted. Yet the treatment meted out to him and his fellow inmates may indeed seem little better than a form of torture:

> We were detained in cell number four, a stretch of about 40 by 100 feet [12 x 30m]. The cell had a capacity of 500 inmates but was congested with prisoners, many of whom slept in pairs under the bed or on the narrow pathways. Water supply to the cell was only about 30 minutes per day while the small amount of food made it compulsory for the inmates to scramble and fight for both food and water. All air-conditioning was switched off from 8.00 a.m. to about 5.00 p.m. so that the cell was automatically turned into an oven during the day and a fridge during the night.

The truth is that taking away a prisoner's freedom has never seemed sufficiently harsh a punishment in itself – either to the medieval king or the modern dictator, or, for that matter, to any number of law-abiding citizens convinced that prison is 'a holiday camp'. Accordingly, a long series of measures have been introduced over time to make physical hardship and discomfort active components of the prison regime.

In England King Edward I introduced the idea of prison *forte et dure* (a strong, hard prison) in 1280. Up until then, those accused of crimes could avoid being tried and punished for them simply by remaining silent and refusing to plead guilty or not guilty before the judge. The new regime, while stopping short of active torture – illegal under the English system – created conditions sufficiently unpleasant to concentrate the mind. The prisoner was locked in a small, dark cell and given a strict bread-and-water diet so meagre as to assure eventual death by starvation.

A collection of relics from the Bastille and other French prisons hints at the tortures awaiting within. Yet none, perhaps, is more chilling than the engraving's central image, the prison door itself, the portal to pain – and, only too frequently, a departure from earthly existence.

King Louis XI of France has to stoop to address his prisoner, Cardinal Balue, whom he kept like an animal in this cage from 1469 to 1480. Apart from its extreme discomfort, such confinement clearly represented a calculated insult to the authority of the Church.

There were other ways of assuring cooperation, such as the very close confinement afforded by a truly tiny cell. In the Tower of London, the notorious chamber known as 'Little Ease' guaranteed the unfortunate inmate just that. Measuring $1.2m^2$ (4sq ft), its cramped conditions prevented the prisoner from ever finding a comfortable position, let alone lying down. Similar dungeons abounded in the castles of Europe. The French *souricière*, or mousehole, measuring only $91cm^2$ (3sq ft), was used up to the end of the 19th century. Even well into the 1920s French prisoners placed in solitary confinement for disciplinary offences would find themselves locked up in cells so small they could touch all four walls at once. The punishment cells in one Romanian prison in the 1940s were a claustrophobic $60cm^2$ (2sq ft).

The discomfort of such cramped quarters was often aggravated by the profound disorientation that resulted from pitch darkness, especially in those medieval dungeons located deep beneath the castle floor where no natural light could penetrate. These conditions have been reproduced in modern prisons, as in the special 'dark cell' in which Chinese dissident Zhu Xiaodan found himself confined for periods of as much as a week at a time. It was, said Zhu, 'a tiny cell, with no light and black walls. There was no sound except for a rushing in my ears ... I felt like I was going crazy.'

A secret interrogation manual, prepared by the American Central Intelligence Agency in 1963, and only made public in 1997 after an application under the Freedom of Information Act made by the *Baltimore Sun*, provides an interesting perspective on Zhu's experiences:

> The more completely the place of confinement eliminates sensory stimuli, the more rapidly and deeply will the interrogatee be affected. Results produced only after weeks or months of imprisonment in an ordinary cell can be duplicated in hours or days in a cell which has no light (or weak artificial light which never varies), which is sound-proofed, in which odors are eliminated, etc. An environment still more subject to control, such as water-tank or iron lung, is even more effective.

Prison authorities down the ages have found other ways of making discomfort a form of torture. Any prisoner held in the Tower of London who heard he was being consigned to the 'Pit', for instance, might well have found himself longing for the relative comfort afforded by 'Little Ease'. Literally a pit, deep down in the very foundations of the Tower, the Pit was situated below the high watermark of the adjacent River Thames. Rats congregated here in their hundreds every day, forced

'The more the place of confinement eliminates sensory stimuli, the more deeply will the interrogatee be affected'

upwards by the rising waters as high tide approached. The hapless prisoner had to fight off these swarming, biting creatures in the darkness. Even if he survived the physical ordeal, his mind was unlikely to remain intact.

Modern gaolers may not have had such gothic punishments at their disposal, but they have still found ways of lending the torment of solitary confinement an extra edge. Simply by washing the floor with dampened chloride of lime, an ordinary cell can be transformed into a chamber of choking, burning fumes. Similar results have been achieved by burning cayenne pepper and puffing the smoke into the cell with bellows. The result is an acrid, stinging cloud that attacks the eyes, nose and throat. Alternatively, prison guards can simply keep up a racket outside a cell to rob the inmate of rest. The British 'Moors Murderer' Ian Brady claimed to have been subjected to such treatment. In one nasty elaboration of this technique, the Dubai Special Branch's 'House of Fun' is fitted up with disco sound and strobe lights, all set to maximum volume; few can endure for very long the pounding cacophony and disorientating light show.

By washing the floor with chloride of lime, a cell can be transformed into a chamber of choking, burning fumes

Still surrender

Close confinement need not, however, be restricted to the dimensions of a prison cell. Many punishment regimes have forced the prisoner to remain immobile of his own accord, as in California's Folsom Prison in the late 19th century. The governor there devised a penalty for recalcitrant prisoners which was simply called 'the spot', a circle of grey paint in the middle of the floor, some 60cm (2ft) in diameter. For as long as his punishment lasted, the prisoner had to stand there motionless for two four-hour stints a day. What may not on the face of it sound a particularly agonizing punishment still proved unpleasant enough for those who endured it. Holding any stationary position for long periods becomes at first exhausting and eventually painful, a fact that torturers have never been slow to use to great effect. Because it involves no elaborate equipment, it is not only highly convenient but also invisible to media watchdogs.

Republican prisoners in the Maze Prison in Northern Ireland, during the worst of 'the troubles', were, for example, made to stand leaning up against walls for hours at a time, their heads hooded, effectively replicating the conditions of the Chinese 'dark cell'. Such torture need leave no traces – no marks on the prisoner, no cell to be seen. The Chinese secret state has long employed similar methods. One political prisoner, Tang, recalled:

One is made to sit on a tiny stool less than 20cm [8in] high on a raised platform of about 90cm² [3sq ft],with back held bolt upright, both feet flat on the floor and hands placed neatly on one's lap. Throughout, one has to look directly at the wall just ahead ...

When Liu Qing, an inmate at Weinan Number Two prison in Shanxi, outraged his guards by smuggling out a manuscript describing his experiences, he was not immediately beaten to the point of death. Instead, his captors played a much longer but cumulatively more devastating game, forcing him to sit stock still on a low bench, without moving or talking, all day and every day for four years. As the CIA's interrogation experts suggested, such treatment makes the prisoner his own torturer:

Whereas pain inflicted on a person from outside himself may actually focus or intensify his will to resist, his resistance is likelier to be sapped by pain that he seems to inflict upon himself ... The immediate source of pain is not the interrogator but the victim himself. The motivational strength of the individual is likely to exhaust itself in this internal encounter.

Pakistani prisoners wear bar shackles in a photograph taken in 1985. Though popularly associated with the dungeons of a luridly-imagined 'medieval' era, such restraints continue in use today, having proved far too useful ever to be discarded.

Inmates at Burma's Rangoon Gaol, 1900, are forced to work the prison's giant treadmill, a machine of extraordinary futility, whose only products were exhausted bodies and broken spirits.

Chains and shackles

Solitary confinement is, of course, an extremely expensive form of incarceration, making demands on space that few penal systems can meet. Most prisoners throughout history have been held in open, communal conditions, with a range of different shackles, fetters and so forth enabling gaolers to keep their charges held close together, as well as stripping them of dignity and, thus, the will to resist. These devices can also serve as horrendous tortures in their own right.

Evidence from around the world confirms that shackles and leg-locks are still very much in use, but the massive clanking chains of popular imagination have to a large extent been consigned to the past. 'Bilboes' were hinged iron rings attached by chains of varying lengths to a bar fixed on the prison floor, allowing minimal freedom of movement. They were named after the Spanish city of Bilbao by an English penal system always quick to attribute its own barbarisms to Spain.

Much the same went for the 'Spanish Collar', a hollow, hinged neck–ring of iron some 7.5cm (3in) deep and 2.5cm (1in) or so thick. Locked or riveted into position, it weighed a crippling 4.5kg (10lb), which could be increased dramatically when the spaces inside were filled with lead. Sharp spikes on the outside ensured that the weary wearer would not be tempted to let his head sag forward on to his chest for respite. Collars used on Jamaican slaves in the 1830s had points over 45cm (18in) long, making any sort of rest out of the question.

The 18th-century murderess Mary Blandy, in prison awaiting execution for the murder of her father, is pictured in contemporary engravings sipping tea with visitors like any genteel hostess. You have to look hard, below the hem of her long dress, to see the iron fetters restricting her movements. By their constant rubbing, they would very likely have inflicted considerable pain. The raw wounds produced by heavy irons were also an open invitation to serious infection in the filth of the typical prison. One unfortunate parliamentary prisoner in Civil War England was severely punished by his royalist gaoler after attempting to escape:

> Smith laid him in irons, hands and feet, and so keepes him about eight weeks; by reason of this cruell usage, he fell very weak and sick, and in his sicknesse he would not suffer anyone to come to help him in his great extremity, so that for three weeks he lay in his owne dung and pisse, and so by a long and languishing disease, being pined to nothing, in a great deale of woe ended his days.

These sort of instruments were used by gaolers to control groups of potentially violent prisoners, and to discipline particular individuals. A cooperative prisoner might be left completely unencumbered, for instance, and a particularly difficult one weighted more heavily. For more cynical warders, however, the appeal of 'ironing' went beyond administrative convenience, being a welcome source of supplementary income in its own right. Bizarrely, fetters and shackles were regarded as 'extras' in prison. Violent and disruptive prisoners (or those deemed to be so by their gaolers) were expected to pay both for the 'privilege' of wearing them and for their eventual removal.

As late as 1916, prisoners who attempted to escape from Onondaga County Penitentiary near Syracuse, New York, were shackled with loads of up to 7kg (16lb) 24 hours a day, for months at a time. Well into the

For more cynical warders, the appeal of 'ironing' went beyond administrative convenience

mid-20th century, meanwhile, 'chain-gangs' worked shackled together on America's roads. Though the great clanking irons of old have endured in some countries where they are used specifically as punishments, shackles are still used for restraint today, although they tend to be much lighter. Their continued use, even in democratic states, was highlighted in 1996 in the UK, where the government admitted with some embarrassment that women prisoners taken to maternity hospitals outside the prison system were being chained up throughout labour to prevent any possibility of escape.

The notion that prison should be an orderly realm of regimentation is a comparatively modern one

In fact such irons have succeeded in outliving the 'punishment jacket' introduced in the 19th century specifically as a more humane alternative. Essentially a broad, thick envelope of canvas and cord thrown round the unruly inmate and then tied up tightly to prevent any movement of the arms, which were tucked up against the chest, this strange garb did indeed offer reformist prison officials an escape from the 'barbaric', medieval connotations of the old irons. Yet its 9cm (3½in) metal collar could rub as viciously as any iron. It was maddeningly frustrating for the wearer, especially when, as was often the case, he was strapped in a standing position to a wall. Prisoners 'on punishment' might spend entire days like this. One 15-year-old boy in the 1850s was driven to suicide by repeated bouts of this torture. Its use in prisons died out in the early 20th century, although the similarly conceived 'straitjacket' was used in mental hospitals long after that.

Mob rule

Thrown into London's Poultry Compter for debt in 1598, the playwright Thomas Dekker was most powerfully struck by the sheer noise:

> ... jailers hoarsely and harshly bawling for prisoners to their bed, and prisoners reviling and cursing jailers for making such a hellish din. Then to hear some in their chambers singing and dancing, being half drunk; others breaking open doors to get more drink to be whole drunk. Some roaring for tobacco; others raging and bidding plague on all tobacco ...

The notion that prison should be an orderly realm of regimentation is a comparatively modern one, and even then it has been something of an ideal. From medieval times through to the early 18th century, the vast majority of prisoners were not set apart in cells under careful supervision but herded together and largely left to themselves. London's purpose-built Newgate prison was legendary for its squalor and moral

turpitude. Through much of the 18th century, accommodation designed to hold 150 prisoners housed at least 250, along with their families and even their pets. Only meagre, poor-quality food rations were provided by the prison authorities, so prisoners had to fend for themselves as best they could. If they had the money, they could pay their keeper to supply fresh food at a hefty mark-up. Beds and bedding also had to be paid for: the keeper was not directly a servant of the state, but bought a franchise to what he then proceeded to run as a business concern. He was motivated by profit and would have made no claim to reforming zeal.

Sullen as they may seem, these English villagers were here in a spirit of heritage and humour. By the time this photograph was taken, in 1895, use of this punishment had long since been consigned to history.

Part punishment, part public proclamation, part popular festivity, the pillory fulfilled a highly complex social role, which is captured vividly here in an engraving by William Henry Pyne (1805).

This was not an environment in which anyone could be expected to thrive, yet male prisoners generally brought their wives and children to serve their sentences with them. What else were they to do, with no social security system to support them in the outside world? The risks of physical and sexual abuse were obvious, though. Rape was routine in such conditions, whether by other inmates or by the gaolers themselves. Prison was generally no place for the puritan: drink was readily available (another source of income for the gaoler) and, with little else to occupy the time, gambling was rife. Women imprisoned for prostitution had every incentive to continue to work inside, while others would, in desperation, hire themselves out for pennies to buy food. Those convicted of capital offences would hope to cheat the waiting hangman's rope by getting themselves pregnant. It was not only food that had to be provided by the prisoners. Funds had to be raised by the inmates to purchase candles, coal and other necessities. The raising of 'garnish', a semi-official tax levied on newly arrived prisoners, was a licence for groups of hardened old lags to rob and extort from the vulnerable. The authorities were happy enough disregard such behaviour – this kind of gang law did, after all, impose a discipline of sorts.

Whenever large groups of potentially dangerous men are crowded together in prison, their keepers will always be tempted to let them police themselves. In the prisons of the United States, horrific violence and abuse are endemic, apparently meeting with little or no resistance from the authorities. 'As the prison population grows, average sentences become longer and mega-prisons of 5000 inmates become the norm', writes American criminologist Christian Parenti. 'Prison gangs – the secret, racialised, micro-governments of the inmate's world – become all the more central to how penitentiaries function.' The authorities do not openly approve of the gangs' activities, of course, but the fact still remains that the gang structure, with its hierarchical pecking order, makes a large mass of dangerous men much easier to manage. A Louisiana guard explained the thinking.

> There are prison administrators who use inmate gangs to help manage the prison. Sex and human bodies become the coin of the realm. Is inmate 'X' writing letters to the editor of the local newspaper and filing lawsuits? Or perhaps he threw urine or feces on an employee? 'Well, Joe, you and Willie and Hank work him over, but be sure you don't break any bones and send him to hospital. If you do a good job, I'll see that you get the blondest boy in the next shipment.'

Mental health clinician Robert Dumond, of the Massachusetts Department of Corrections, estimates that the chances of a young prisoner's chances of avoiding rape in an adult prison are 'almost zero … He'll get raped within the first 24 or 48 hours. That's almost standard.' Around 290,000 male inmates are raped in American prisons every year, claims the pressure group Stop Prisoner Rape – many of them raped not once or twice, but daily. One prisoner, 23-year-old Eddie Dillard, transferred to California's Security Housing Unit for kicking a female guard, was placed in a cell with one Wayne Robertson, the 'Booty Bandit'. Dillard's protests that his cellmate was a known predator were overruled. The guards then proceeded to look the other way for several days while Dillard was beaten, raped and tortured repeatedly.

If men are raped by their fellow inmates, women prisoners are raped too, but by their guards. The 1996 Human Rights Watch report on rape by male officers in women's prisons in America covered only five states, yet ran to 350 pages. In 1998, five female former inmates of Dublin, California, won damages after their guards were found to have pimped them out to male inmates of the prison. Even if the state does not officially sanction such abuses, surely the placement of vulnerable prisoners in an abusive prison culture is, at the very least, conniving with a sort of torture.

The gang structure, with its pecking order, makes a large mass of dangerous men much easier to manage

The isolated soul

The search for an approach to imprisonment that offers inmates something more constructive than torture by brutishness and squalor has been a long and, in many ways, frustrating one. The movement began in the West with the Enlightenment of the 18th century, when a new mood of optimism about human potential went hand in hand with a deep distaste for what came to be seen as the barbarities of old. Writers and philosophers like Voltaire and Rousseau wrote scathingly of a Europe enslaved in benighted superstition, cruel social practices and despotic rule. 'Man was born free,' wrote Rousseau, 'and everywhere he is in chains.' No better proof of this could be found than in Europe's prisons: squalid sumps into which the abandoned dregs of society were flushed. In the right conditions, with the right care, attention and education, might not these lost souls realize their innate capacity for good?

If the trouble with traditional prisons was the promiscuity in which inmates lived, and their lack of supervision by cynical staff, all that was now to be brought to an end. In Philadelphia, in the Quaker state of Pennsylvania, the first great 'penitentiary', Eastern State, was opened in 1829 – so called for the penitence it was designed to instil in its inmates. Prisoners were stripped of their identity upon arrival, allocated a number and a solitary cell. No contact with fellow inmates was allowed. In such intense isolation, the thinking went, the wretched criminal's thoughts would turn inward and he would begin to meditate upon the wrongs he had done.

There could be no doubt that the penitentiary represented a big step forward in material comfort. Yet, in its sheer unrelenting isolation from society and stimulus, the penitentiary's approach was, as the London Times surmised, positively 'maniac-making'. While dignitaries came from all over the world to marvel at what was promoted as a utopian project, the English novelist Charles Dickens, who was given a conducted tour in 1842, was altogether less impressed. He commented:

> The system is rigid, strict and hopeless, and I believe it to be cruel and wrong. I hold this slow and daily tampering with the mysteries of the brain, to be immeasurably worse than any torture of the body.

Despite such reservations, the penitentiary plan was embraced enthusiastically by policy-makers abroad. London's Pentonville Prison, opened in 1842, was a clear copy of Eastern State, and was in turn the model for a further 50-odd British prisons – many of which remain in use today. The penitentiary system would eventually be undermined by

With the right care, attention and education, might not these lost souls realise their innate capacity for good?

human nature – not only the age-old refusal of sinners to repent when pressured to do so, but also the reluctance of hard-pressed civic authorities to pour ever more resources into the 'care' of offenders.

Where spiritual contemplation had been seen to fail, might not the Protestant work ethic succeed? The first treadmill, invented by William Cubitt, had been installed in London's Brixton Prison in 1817. Up to 40 prisoners standing side by side trod what resembled an elongated water wheel in Brixton. In Pentonville, in line with penitentiary principles, they were screened from one another as they worked in wooden stalls. Prisoners performed alternating bouts of 15 minutes on and 15 minutes off, with 15 such shifts in each working day. The treadmill was not only gruelling but dangerous, since the slightest lapse of concentration could

The pillory's happiest hour? Sentenced to the 'punishment' in London in 1704, the author Daniel Defoe is showered, not with dead rats and dirt, but with compliments and flowers, by a crowd who supported his satirical stand against the government.

A threefold cangue yokes three convicted criminals together in this photograph taken in China in the 1890s.

cause a painful fall as the wheel turned inexorably on and on. And the product of all this labour? A windmill-shaped fan on the roof turned round and round. 'Grinding the wind', the prisoners called it. As an exercise in futility, the treadmill was arguably surpassed by a later innovation, the 'crank'. This was a stiff, cranked handle protruding from an iron drum, its inner mechanism consisting of a series of scoops on a rotating wheel. These picked up sand from the bottom of the drum as they turned, emptying it out again as they reached the top. A prisoner sentenced to a regime of 'hard labour' was expected to complete 10,000 revolutions every working day, each religiously recorded by a meter on the machine. This was indeed hard labour, as the report of a government committee pointed out:

> We were assured that, in order to accomplish such a task ... a boy would necessarily exert a force equal to one fourth of the ordinary work of a draught horse; the average estimate of the work of a boy, in ordinary labour out of a prison, being about one tenth of the same; and, indeed, that no human being, whether adult or juvenile, could continue to perform such an amount of labour of this kind for several consecutive days, especially on a prison diet, without wasting much and suffering greatly.

Despite these official reservations, inmates who failed to complete their allotted task in the time allowed were forced to continue working without food – regardless of youth, advanced age or poor health. In their efforts to avoid the brutalities of old, prison reformers had instead created a physical and mental torture of another kind.

Ritual shaming

Prison is not the only arena in which punishment can take the form of torture. In the past, a range of different punishments made public examples of miscreants without actually locking them up. The stocks of medieval Europe, a form of outdoor imprisonment, had been used centuries beforehand. Though the word itself came from the Anglo-Saxon 'stocce', for plank or tree-trunk, similar lockable hinged boards, with holes for the ankles and/or the wrists, had held down such Old Testament figures as Job and the prophet Jeremiah during their persecutions, as well as the disciples Paul and Silas in the Acts of the Apostles. In the England of the Middle Ages, the stocks were a key feature on a town's central green or at a crossroads – even when empty, a powerful symbol of the rule of law.

The typical stocks could accommodate two prisoners at once – an adulterous couple, say, or, for that matter, a man and wife who persistently argued. In some places, however, much bigger versions were to be found, for example the stocks at Saffron Walden, Essex, where five malefactors could be held simultaneously by both wrists and feet. Tradesmen and -women who short-changed their customers or sold substandard goods, incorrigible drunks, 'loose' women or vagrants; and

In the England of the Middle Ages, the stocks were a key feature – even when empty, a powerful symbol of the rule of law

even persistent swearers might find themselves subjected to a spell in the stocks. As a rule the offender spent only six hours or less locked up, though it could be far longer. Periods of days and even weeks have been recorded. In any case, the 'lightest' sentence might turn out to be far more severe if the attendant crowd, whose crowing, jeering presence was of course a vital part of the punishment, was in the mood to make life difficult for the victim. Pinned down in the stocks, the victim was effectively defenceless not only against public derision, but any missiles the crowd felt like hurling, or, indeed, any beating it might wish to administer.

The purpose of the pillory was, of course, precisely to render the victim vulnerable to such attack, his face held up as a target, his wrists tightly trapped to preclude any possibility of self-defence. More of an urban phenomenon than the stocks was the pillory, which was most

Simultaneously imprisoned, exhibited – and, ultimately, executed – Chinese prisoners of the early twentieth century could be kept in 'death cages' while they slowly starved.

often to be found at important city crossroads, where minor offenders would be exposed to the ridicule or the wrath of their fellow citizens. While the stooped position and the tight champing of the board-yoke at the neck must have made any stint in the pillory extremely uncomfortable at best, the essence of the punishment lay in the reaction of the crowd.

Pilloried in London in 1704 for an incautious satire on the government, the author Daniel Defoe found himself lionised by a like-minded cockney crowd who plied him with food and drink, cheering him to the skies and showering the pillory with flowers. This was very much the exception to the rule, however. Rotten fruit and vegetables, bad eggs, dead rats and dogs as well as animal and human excrement were all liable to be hurled. When the salvoes included stones, the results could be far more deadly. In 1732, for instance, John Waller, a robber and perjurer, died of injuries sustained in the pillory, while in 1751 two other robbers died in the same way.

A punishment that seems largely to have been reserved for women was the thew, much in use in medieval England. Essentially a simple neck-ring chained to a post, the thew might also feature a raised platform to hold the offender up for public disapprobation – or bombardment. It is not clear whether it can be regarded as a crude predecessor to the pillory proper, but its function was certainly similar. In 1364, for instance, alewife Alice de Caustone was found to have defrauded customers by selling beer in 'quart pots' with thick false bottoms. She was, says the record, 'punnyshed by the pyllorie of the thew for women'. The 'finger stocks' found in old manor houses and country churches held the miscreant prisoner by a single finger, a device calculated to produce humiliation rather than serious pain. Light-fingered or surly servants or lax attenders at church might be paraded ignominiously in these stocks.

Like other old tortures, the stocks and pillory saw service in the colonies long after they had been deemed unacceptable in Britain. The 'field stocks' of the West Indies were introduced for insubordinate female slaves once regulations to prohibit whipping had come into force in the mid-19th century. The wrist restraints on these stocks could be adjusted so that the slave's arms were stretched high above her head, and she was forced to stand on tiptoe for long hours at a time, all her body weight thrown on to her toes and wrists, which might be further weighted with lead or iron – if such was the overseer's whim.

Thousands of miles away, meanwhile, the pillory had its Asian equivalent in the Chinese cangue, a wide wooden board through which the offender's head and hands were yoked. Though not fixed into the

The stocks and pillory saw service in the colonies long after they had been deemed unacceptable in Britain

earth like the western pillory, the cangue was ungainly and uncomfortable, and above all obvious, especially when the victim was paraded through the streets, his crime proclaimed by scrolls attached to the woodwork.

Another form of public exhibition was the cage: a barred or slatted cage in which minor offenders were displayed to a disapproving public. In 18th-century Newcastle-upon-Tyne in England, prostitutes were showered with dirt and excrement as they were paraded naked in wheeled cages around the town. This punishment had its origins in the wars of the Middle East and Central Asia, when a city's captors would quell the defeated populace by stripping leading citizens naked and cramming them into cages, which were then hung from the walls. The cage occupants were left to hunger, thirst and bake in the midday sun. Many in continental Europe would meet a similar fate as late as the 18th century – left to starve as they swung in wind, rain, snow and scorching summer sun, in cages suspended from gibbets or from city or cathedral walls. The cages' narrow, iron bars forced the victims to remain standing right to the point of unconsciousness and, inevitably, death. Even then, they were robbed of any dignity as their bodies were left to decay for months on end.

One punishment was used exclusively for women: the branks or 'scold's bridle', by which headstrong women, or 'shrews', were tamed in 17th – and 18th-century Britain. Since Quaker women insisted on preaching in the streets, giving offence both by their unfeminine behaviour and their doctrinal message, they too would often be singled out for this treatment. (Ironically, a variant of this torture, the 'iron gag', helped to maintain the deep spiritual silence of Philadelphia's Quaker-inspired Eastern State Penitentiary in the 19th century.) The branks consisted of an iron muzzle with an iron plate specifically designed to hold down the tongue. Victims may have been led like bridled beasts through the streets, but humiliation was only half of it. The tongue plate was often fitted with sharp, downward-thrusting spikes capable of inflicting agonising pain at the slightest movement of the tongue or jerk of the halter. Just how frequently the scold's bridle was used cannot be known, but it does seem as though every settlement of any size in England and Scotland had one – the city of Chester alone had no fewer than four.

The precise point at which legitimate punishment becomes cruel abuse, or close confinement constitutes torture, is, as we have seen, a matter of difficult debate. What is not in doubt, however, is the incalculable suffering endured by men and women throughout the ages, from dangerous murderers to mere nagging 'scolds'.

Victims may have been led like bridled beasts through the streets, but humiliation was only the half of it

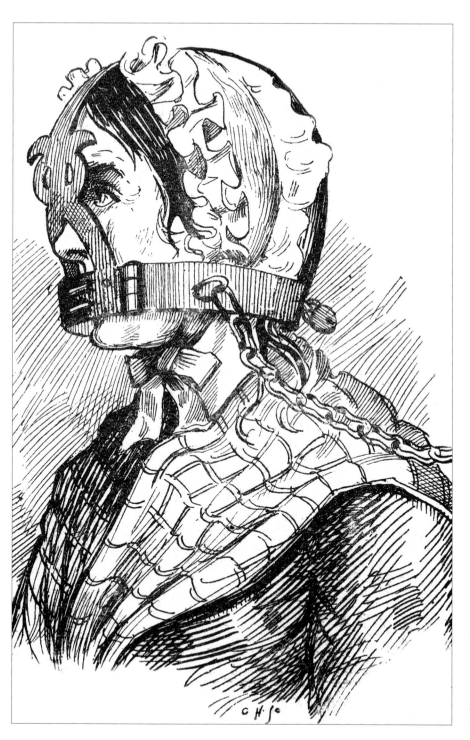

The branks was used to silence 'nagging' women. The spiked steel plates used to hold down the tongue, and the yanking of the cord used to lead her along, guaranteed the victim an excruciating experience.

Chapter Two

Stretching and Suspension

The Greek hero Theseus is most famous for having slain the Minotaur, yet his encounter with the cruel giant Procrustes is also legendary. Procrustes would wait by a lonely roadside, waylaying tired travellers and inviting them to rest on his special bed – a bed that, he said, could accommodate a sleeper of any size. Little did his unfortunate guests imagine that if they were too tall, they would simply be cut to size; if too short, their bodies would be stretched until they fitted to perfection. Theseus was to be Procrustes' last guest, for the hero killed the giant in his bed. But Procrustes and his accursed bed provide the perfect mythological counterpart to the vile, and all too real, trade of torturers everywhere: shattering the mind and crushing the spirit by means of contorting, twisting and breaking the body.

The rack

The Procrustean bed finds its perfect analogy in the rack, on which for many centuries torture victims found themselves stretched. The Greek dramatist Aristophanes refers to its use in classical times. Though some racks seem to have been circular, the victim stretched out upon the revolving rim, most racks looked like some macabre parody of the bed of ease. The victim would be lain on the floor within a rectangular wooden framework, his hands firmly bound and stretched out above his head, with both hands and feet anchored by weights – or, later, more often rollers. Levers at each end of the bed loosened or tightened the cords that held the prisoner's extremities, lifting him up slowly until he hung in the air before his questioners.

In later versions of this evolving technology, transverse struts across the frame were used to lift the victim to a convenient height for the torturer, earning the contraption its Spanish name, the *escalera*, or ladder. (The name seems particularly apt, given the tendency in Spanish torture chambers for the rack to be installed, vertically, against a wall.) A further refinement substituted spiked or studded rollers for these wooden struts, making the machine run that much more smoothly – and painfully. In an Italian variation, a sharp spike was set right beneath the

A suspected witch is put to the test in this 16th-century engraving, her body pulled every which way by a cunning refinement of the punishment of the pulley.

victim's back, thereby adding to his many agonies the urgent necessity of keeping his back tensed and well clear. The spike was mockingly known as *la veglia*, or 'vigilance'. The 'Austrian ladder' leaned up against a wall at an angle, and differed from the conventional rack in that the victim's whole body was not actually stretched, only the arms. The turning mechanism drew the wrists slowly upwards until both shoulders were dislocated.

Even without these variations, the conventional rack was quite destructive enough. As the interrogator plied his prisoner with questions, up to four assistants worked the screws, while ratcheted rollers allowed tension to be maintained between successive turns. Whether operated by four men or just one, the rack stretched its victim's

Though speculative in its details, this 19th-century artist's impression of the rack used by Roman legionaries to torture Gallic prisoners is as good a guess as any – and by no means implausible in its technical sophistication.

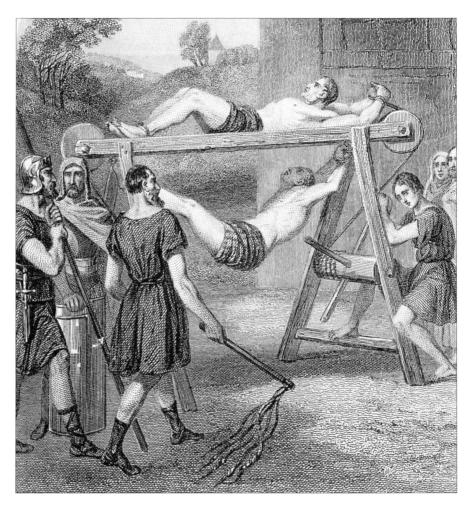

body to breaking point. First the arms and then the legs gave way as joints were dislocated and ligatures torn. Moreover, with arms and legs splayed out and firmly anchored, the prisoner's face and body were open to any other injury his persecutors cared to inflict: No mere instrument of pain in its own right, the rack was effectively the torturer's workbench.

According to John Foxe's *Book of Martyrs*, a famous 16th-century account of those martyred by pagan – and later by papist – oppressors, Quintinus, one of the early Christian martyrs, experienced the rack's multiple agonies while being tortured by pagan persecutors:

> Then the Prefect, raging with despotic fury, ordered the holy Quintinus to be so cruelly racked at the pulleys that his limbs were forced apart at the joints from sheer violence … he commanded him to be beaten with small cords, and boiling oil and pitch and melted fat to be poured over him, that no kind of punishment or torment might fail to add to his bodily anguish.

How accurate Foxe could be about such details, so many centuries later, is of course open to some degree of doubt. The description may in fact be a better guide to 16th- and 17th-century practice than to that of the early part of the First Millennium. And it does seem to have been in Reformation Europe that the rack really came into its own, against the backdrop of mounting religious conflict.

By the time the Englishman John Coustos – suspected of freemasonry – fell prisoner to the Portuguese Inquisition at Lisbon in 1743, operators of the rack had clearly attained a certain virtuosity. Having first been stripped and placed on the rack, his neck in an iron collar, his feet secured by a pair of rings, Coustos found his arms and legs being looped round with thin ropes passed through apertures in the rack's framework from below. These ropes were evidently connected to screws underneath the stretching surface, for they were now tightened, cutting into Coustos's legs and arms with agonizing pain and sending the blood spurting as they sank deep into his flesh. Four times the Inquisition's servants turned the screws, until the ropes penetrated to the bone and Coustos lost consciousness. He was then released from the rack and granted a full six weeks' remission – not out of pity, but so that his body might be fully fit to be tortured all over again.

His tormentors tried a new approach on returning Coustos to the rack. This time they stretched out his hands, palms outwards, and tied his wrists, before cranking cords were used to pull his hands gradually

Four times the Inquisition's servants turned the screws, until the ropes penetrated to the bone and Coustos lost consciousness

together behind him until the backs touched. Again and again, the process was repeated, until Coustos's arms slipped from their shoulder sockets, and blood oozed from his mouth. Taken back to his cell once more, he was tended by surgeons, restoring his body for another bout on the rack. Two months later he was adjudged ready for torture once more. This time a thick chain of iron was looped twice round his body, across the stomach, and then bound by rings at both ends to his wrists. These rings were in turn connected to pulleys on either side, which his torturers worked by means of a roller. As the ropes were gradually tightened, the pressure was increased on the chain around Coustos's body until it cut deep into his flesh while simultaneously dislocating his wrists and shoulders. Yet again, he was taken away to be tended to, and, a few weeks later, brought back to the rack once more. Again, however, the Inquisition's best efforts proved of no avail, and they finally gave up in disgust. Coustos was sentenced to serve four years as a galley slave.

Two months later he was adjudged ready for torture once more

An earlier prisoner of the Inquisition, the Scottish traveller William Lithgow, had also experienced the rack's adaptability when he was arrested as a spy in Málaga, Spain, in 1620. The rack on which he was placed was not set out horizontally like a table, but upright against a wall, a position that increased the machine's sheer violence, while limiting the torturer's ability to fine-tune his victim's sufferings. No matter, because in this instance it was not this function of the rack that was being used, as Lithgow himself recalled:

I was by the executioner stripped to the skin, brought to the rack, and then mounted by him on the top of it, where soon after I was hung by the bare shoulders with two small cords, which went under both my arms, running on two rings of iron that were fixed in the wall above my head. Thus being hoisted to the appointed height, the tormenter descended below, and drawing down my legs, through the two sides of the three-planked rack, he tied a cord about each of my ankles and then ascending upon the rack he drew the cords upward, and bending forward with main force my two knees against the two planks, the sinews of my hams burst asunder, and the lids of my knees being crushed, and the cords made fast, I hung so demained for a large hour ... Then the tormenter did cast a cord over both arms seven distant times: and then lying down upon his back, and setting both his feet on my hollow pinched belly, he charged and drew violently with his hands, making my womb suffer the force of his feet, till the seven several cords combined in one place of my arme (and cutting the sinews and flesh to the bare bones) did pull in my fingers close to the palm of my hands; the left hand of which is lame so still and will be for ever...

In God's name

No organization looms larger in the history of torture than the Inquisition, an institution that brought together the repressive force of both church and state in an attempt to put down any religious or political opposition. With the right to arrest and interrogate whomsoever they chose, the Inquisition's authority quickly outstripped that of local bishops and clergy. And, like all great institutions, it was in no hurry to surrender any of its accumulated powers. By 1252, those powers included the right to torture suspects in certain situations – for example, when a suspect denied a charge of heresy that was attested to by others (by widespread rumour if not by individual witnesses), or when an accused was inconsistent in his answers under interrogation.

Who can tell how closely the Inquisition adhered to the strict regulations supposedly governing its use of torture? Our experience of human nature suggests that, once granted, such licence is only too readily abused. Like all agencies that deploy torture, the Inquisition could always justify its behaviour to the satisfaction of its own supporters: Were not those heretics who were forced to recant doing themselves an eternal favour? And for every body racked, think how many wayward souls would be frightened into conformity, and thus salvation. Why should the inquisitor not sleep easy in his bed? The 'proof' of the Inquisition's value was evident in the admissions of heresy it managed to wring from the accused.

Rack technology was streamlined through the Middle Ages and Renaissance, ratcheting gears allowing one man to operate instruments of torture. Studded rollers add to the agony of this model favoured in Germany, but its chief advantage to the torturer was its convenience.

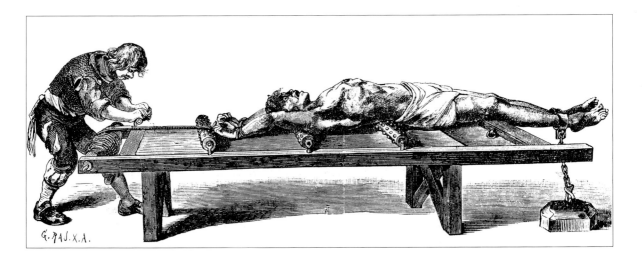

G. RAJ. X. A.

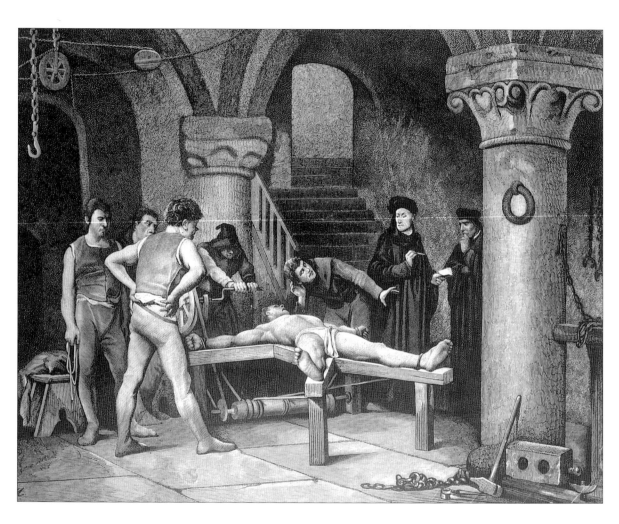

Held spreadeagled on a wooden X, this prisoner is not stretched as he would be on the conventional rack; rather, the engine slowly tightens lacerating cords around his wrists and ankles.

The Inquisition could be said to have come of age in the early 14th century with the campaign against the Knights Templars. An armed order established in the 12th century to protect Christian pilgrims in the Holy Land, the Knights Templar had carved out a position as courier and banker to the Church at large. By the end of the 13th Century, their wealth and power had increased to such an extent that even Rome became nervous. Accordingly, from 1307, Pope Clement used the Inquisition to attack the order, accusing its leaders of all manner of sacrilege and satanic rites. As time went on, the Inquisition found more and more hidden heresies to contend with throughout western Europe, and it dealt with them as rigorously as it knew how, employing torture as its ultimate sanction. It is debatable just how effective a sanction it was in the end, given that it seems to have been used most freely of all in Germany, the land of Martin Luther, where Rome's authority would finally be defied once and for all with the establishment of the Protestant Church.

The Spanish Inquisition

In Spain, the Inquisition was late getting under way, though it would finally come together with a vengeance. Heresy had not been so much of a problem here in the medieval period, for Christians had been bound together by the need to repel a common enemy. Ever since the Iberian kingdom of the Visigoths had been invaded by the Islamic Moors in the 8th century, Christian Spain – initially corralled in a tiny pocket in the north of Spain – had been slowly pushing its way southwards again. By the late 15th century, a Spain more or less united by the marriage of Ferdinand of Aragon and Isabella of Castile could envisage 'one last push' that might see the triumph of Christianity complete. It was in this context that, in 1478, the 'Catholic Monarchs' called the Spanish Inquisition into being.

In the south, where Muslims, Christians and Jews had for so long lived harmoniously side by side, Muslims were driven out, while Jews were offered the starkest of choices: to accept conversion, or face exile, even death. Inevitably, many converted without conviction, quietly pursuing their ancestral ways. The task of rooting out any such recidivism fell to the Inquisition. In both Spain proper and in 'New Spain', the Spanish colonies of Latin America, anyone suspected of practising Judaism might be forced to confess on the rack or potror, their throats encased in garrotes. These were metal hoops which encircled the neck. When tightened they drove spikes into the victim's throat.

Legacy of the rack

As many an English 'recusant' could testify, such cruelty was not a monopoly of the Catholic Church. During the religious ferment that gripped England in the 16th century, the rack was used freely not only by the Catholic Queen Mary, but by those monarchs who had broken with Rome. The English 'recusants' were supposed converts – in this case to the Anglican Church – who secretly adhered to the Roman rite. They would have found the rack in the Tower of London quite as painful as any in Spain or the wider Catholic world. Supposedly introduced to England in 1420, by the then Constable of the Tower, the Duke of Exeter, torture on the rack would subsequently be known, in the blackest sort of humour, as being 'married to the Duke of Exeter's

The rack was used freely not only by the Catholic Queen Mary, but also by those monarchs who had broken with Rome

daughter'. Lord High Treasurer Lord Burghley may have claimed in 1583 that the Queen's servants were charged to use the rack 'in as charitable manner as such a thing might be', but many hundreds of men and women would find this of little comfort.

Though the rack itself is now confined to the fair or theme park chamber of horrors, the basic idea lives on in the 'German chair' still used by torturers in Syria. Its moveable backrest is progressively lowered, slowly extending the spine and exerting intense pressure on the neck and limbs, eventually causing asphyxiation and loss of consciousness, and ultimately, of course, the fracturing of the vertebrae.

Such sophisticated machinery is not necessarily needed to recreate the effects of the old-fashioned rack: There is, for example, the technique of *cheera*, or 'tearing', which is so popular with the Indian security forces. Simply by holding the suspect down and forcing his legs further and further apart, they can cause tearing to muscles – with terrible, burning pain – and, finally, dislocation. Though the joints are afterwards replaced, they will never be quite the same again, and many victims are unable to walk without pain for many years afterwards.

> *The Queen's servants were charged to use the rack 'in as charitable a manner as such a thing might be'*

Manacles and pulleys

When in 1605, their abortive 'Gunpowder Plot' blew up in their faces and Guido 'Guy' Fawkes and his fellow-conspirators failed to bring down the English Parliament, they were sent to the torture chamber so that any accomplices might be discovered. Before being dispatched to the rack, however, Fawkes seems to have been put to a 'gentler torture' on King James I's orders. This is widely assumed to have meant the 'manacles' or 'gauntlets', iron wrist restraints fixed high up on a wall. The restraints were fitted on the wrists and savagely tightened by means of a screw. Then the stool or block on which the prisoner stood was kicked away, leaving him dangling in increasing discomfort for hours at a time. One victim recalled:

> the chief pain [was] in my breast, belly, arms, and hands. I thought that all the blood in my body had run into my arms, and began to burst out of my finger ends. This was a mistake: but the arms swelled, till the gauntlets were buried within the flesh. After being thus suspended an hour, I fainted: and when I came to myself, I found the executioners supporting me in their arms: they replaced the pieces of wood under my feet, but as soon as I recovered, removed them again. Thus I continued hanging for the space of five hours, during which I fainted eight or nine times.

In this woodcut, thought to date from 1541, a prisoner endures the torture of the strappado before his inquisitor. A rope is passed around his wrists and slowly tightened as an additional refinement to his suffering.

Whether Guy Fawkes even made it to the rack is far from clear – though the hand in which he signed the record of testimony famously grew shakier by the day. The manacles alone, for all their 'gentleness', could have done that damage. The effect of a severe manacling is much the same as that of the rack. Indeed, both seek to subdue the spirit by stretching the body; the major difference is that the manacles rely on the force of gravity.

Relying on the same effect, the pulley or garrucha was, after the rack, the favoured torture of the Inquisition. The pulley offered a sliding scale of pain for the experienced tormentor, involving both simple squassation and its excruciating refinement, *strappado*. For squassation, the victim's ankles were bound together to prohibit movement, while the wrists were tied tightly behind his back, and another longer rope fastened by one end to this bond and passed over a hook in the ceiling. His tormentors could then pull on the rope to hoist him high into the air where he hung in agony, suspended by his wrists, his shoulders straining at their sockets.

This technique is still very much in use among torturers today. In China it is known as the 'hanging aeroplane' for obvious reasons. The practice is often called 'Palestinian hanging' in the Middle East – Amnesty International reports that interrogation rooms in Iran and Turkey are equipped with hooks for this specific purpose. Whoever is administering the torture, in whatever historical epoch, the sensations felt by the victim are the same: terrible pain in the shoulders, which, within a few hours, can result in fainting.

Torturers do not always want to wait this long. The Inquisition developed a number of variations on the basic technique. In the first

A hanging position such as this one, captured in a Chinese watercolour of around 1900, served not only to stretch the body painfully, but to leave the victim helplessly exposed to further tortures.

place, the feet might be weighted to increase the agony of stretching. If this failed to get a result, then *strappado* itself might be tried. The rope, having been drawn up to its maximum tension, would be allowed to slip through the executioner's hands a metre or so, causing the victim to fall a split second before suddenly being pulled up short. The result was agonizing; shoulders often became dislocated, while limbs might be torn away entirely.

The Inquisition seems to have had clear rules on what degrees of squassation and strappado were to be used in particular cases: whether the victim should be weighted, for example, whether left simply to hang (and in that case for just how long) or subjected to full strappado. As with the rack, such stretching was seldom much more than an overture: after all, the suspended, naked body was uniquely vulnerable to physical and psychological assault alike. The sickening reality of this is brought home all too graphically in the frank account of 'C.M.', a 17-year-old girl tortured in Turkey in 1995:

Slow strangulation kills this prisoner, the bricks being removed only one by one; he is fed throughout to ensure that he stays alive long enough to suffer.

> I know they wanted to spoil my psychological world, to spoil me, to make me hopeless ... They forced me to take off all my clothes. I always was blindfolded for interrogation and torture. My arms were tied behind my back so that my forearms overlapped, and I was suspended from a bar attached to my arms. It was extremely painful. A wire was attached to one of my toes and another wire applied shocks to different parts of my body: my breasts, feet, abdomen and vagina. During the electricity, they said: 'We know you are guilty, we have decided to make you speak. If not today, tomorrow, or the next day.'

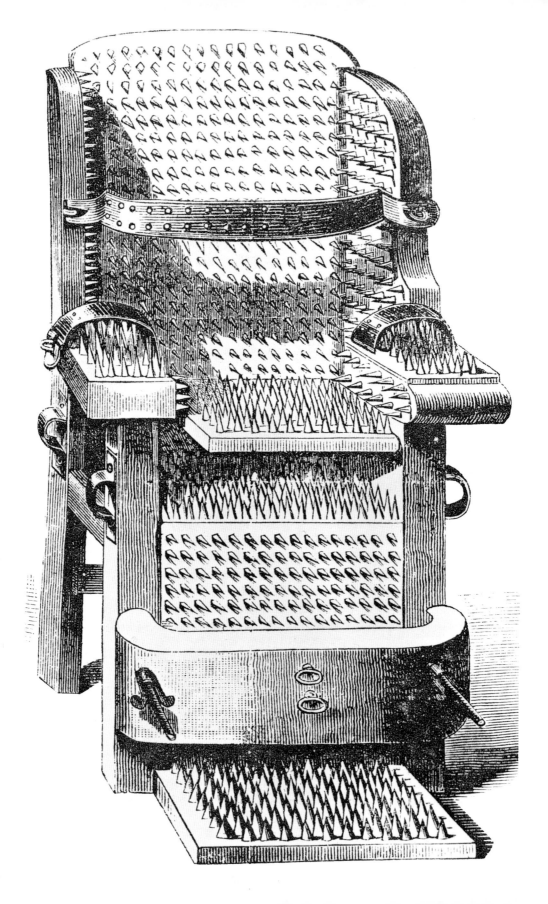

Chapter Three

Applying Pressure

‘Jesu! Jesu! Jesu! Have Mercy on Me!’ These are reported to have been the last words of St Margaret Clitherow, the 'Pearl of York', before she died, crushed beneath a heavy door on which rocks and weights had been heaped. A tradesman's wife who lived in the Shambles, York, she had converted to Catholicism as an adult in 1571 – about as bad a time in English history as can be imagined for such a decision. Far from fearing martyrdom, she seems positively to have welcomed it when it came in 1586. When the judge condemned her to the torture of *peine forte et dure* – strong, hard pain – she had said 'God be thanked, I am not worthy of so good a death', and by all accounts she approached the place of execution in a spirit of serenity. Asked if even at the eleventh hour she would confess her crimes, she smiled joyfully as she said: 'No, no, Mr Sheriff, I die for the love of my Lord Jesu.'

Margaret Clitherow's fate had been shared by many men and women before her. If anything, hers was a comparatively humane version of the punishment *peine forte et dure*, with a death lasting only 15 minutes. Between 360 and 410kg (800 and 900lbs) in weight are said to have been piled upon her, but the sharp stone her executioners placed beneath her back helped break her spine and rupture important internal organs, making for a short if brutal death instead of a lingering agony.

Why did Margaret meet this death, then, rather than the burning at the stake that had been customary for women martyrs? The charge against her was that she had harboured priests in her home, had Mass said there and received the Sacraments. If her case had gone to trial, however, her children and servants would inevitably have been called as witnesses: Their testimony would have sent her to her death, and they would thus have been left with a stain of guilt upon their innocent souls. Rather than allow this to happen, Margaret had chosen not to plead. The *peine forte et dure* to which she was condemned was the automatic punishment in such cases.

Strictly speaking, this 'strong, hard pain' was not a punishment, since no case had been tried and no guilt established. Nor, for that matter, did it technically count as 'torture' – that would have been illegal under English law. The reasoning was that in such situations the accused was never tortured, only 'pressed to plead'. Introduced in around 1406, the punishment of *peine forte et dure* was simply a beefed-up successor to

Anybody forced to sit in the chair depicted in this woodcut from around 1870 effectively underwent assault from every side. Fearsome as its spikes were, the real terror of the chair lay in the crushing pressures brought to bear by its tightening vices.

Edward I's idea of prison *forte et dure*, a method of slow starvation, which was perceived as being a bit too soft. It was also in the Crown's interest to deter the accused from refusing to plead, for its coffers benefitted richly from the confiscated funds of those who were tried and convicted of capital offences.

From the beginning of the 15th century, then, those who remained 'mute of malice', refusing to plead guilty or not guilty to the charge, would be subject to the new compulsion of peine forte et dure. This meant that:

> The criminal is sent back to the prison whence he came, and there laid
> in some low dark room, upon the bare ground on his back, all naked,
> except his privy parts, his arms and legs drawn with cords fastened to

An 18th-century engraving shows the biblical punishment of 'crushing one to pieces under thorns' – though the thorns would presumably have been the merest irritant beside the killing pressure of these great boulders.

several parts of the room; and then there is laid on his body, iron, stone, or lead, so much as he can bear; the next day he shall have three morsels of barley bread, without drink; and the third day shall have to drink some of the kennel water with bread. And this method is in strictness to be observed until he is dead.

So wrote John Stow, the historian of London, in 1598. More than a century later, the practice was still alive. As late as 1721, the *Nottingham Mercury* included in its 'London News' section a report that two highwaymen, Thomas Green, alias Phillips, and Thomas Spiggott, both refusing to plead, had been sentenced to the punishment of the press:

> The former, on sight of the terrible machine, desired to be carried back to the sessions house, where he pleaded not guilty. But the other, who behaved himself very insolently to the ordinary who was ordered to attend him, seemingly resolved to undergo the torture ... but after enduring the punishment for an hour, and having three or four hundredweight put on him, he at last submitted to plead, and was carried back, when he pleaded not guilty.

The prison chaplain witnessed Spiggott's punishment, and his account was later published in the *Annals of Newgate*:

> The chaplain found him lying in the vault upon the bare ground, with 350 pounds' weight upon his breast, and then prayed with him, and at several times asked him why he should hazard his soul by such obstinate kind of self-murder. But all the answer that he made was 'Pray for me; pray for me'. He sometimes lay silent under the pressure as if insensible to the pain, and then again would retch his breath very quick and short. Several times he complained that they had laid a cruel weight upon his face, though it was covered with nothing but a thin cloth, which was afterwards removed and laid more light and hollow; yet he still complained of the prodigious weight upon his face, which might be caused by the blood being forced up thither and pressing the veins so violently ...

It is significant, though, that Spiggott, for all his early defiance, finally capitulated. Though *peine forte et dure* would continue in force until the late 18th century, it was most unusual at this late stage for anybody to be actually crushed to death. The punishment makes its

'The former, on sight of the terrible machine, desired to be carried back to the sessions house, where he pleaded not guilty'

solitary appearance in American history with the case of Salem witch hunt suspect Giles Corey, who was pressed to death in 1692 after he had refused to plead. The last recorded fatality in England appears to have been one Major Strangeways, who, in 1676, was charged with murdering his sister's suitor. He was determined not to plead, apparently to avoid losing his property, and the judge duly condemned him to *peine forte et dure*. The Major himself seems to have treated it as a death sentence, wearing mourning clothes and having his closest friends standing by. They actually seem to have assisted in the execution, piling on weights and when, finally, after ten minutes, the Major still remained alive, stood on the pile of weights themselves to put an end to their friend's great agony.

Perhaps, too, officials and executioners did not have the stomach for the long, drawn-out suffering involved.

This case highlights the way in which the punishment seems to have been modulated in its purpose through its long, cruel history. It began as a long, drawn-out torture, calculated to give the prisoner ample opportunity to reflect on his his refusal not to plead, but with the certainty of death at the end to concentrate the mind. This would obviously suit the state, which stood to gain whenever an accused decided to plead, stood trial and was then found guilty. But, eventually, it became merely a form of execution for those who had defied the system. Perhaps, too, officials and executioners did not themselves have the stomach for the prolonged suffering involved in the full medieval *peine*. By the 16th century, most victims seem to have been meeting their deaths quite quickly. Those examples we have from the 18th century suggest another type of torture again, still grim but generally not fatal – a way of applying pressure – quite literally – to a difficult prisoner.

Torture by pressure of this kind was not confined to Europe. One of Japan's most cruel punishments up to the 19th century was a type of torture by cutting and compression known as 'hugging the stone'. The prisoner, having first been forced to kneel on a board studded with razor-sharp flints, was then made to hold heavy weights heaped up in his lap. Alternatively, they might be piled on the backs of his legs. In parts of the Middle East, according to Amnesty International, the punishment of *peine forte et dure* is still in use today.

The Scavenger's Daughter

This invention was the brainchild of the Lieutenant of the Tower of London in Henry VIII's reign, Sir Leonard Skeffington or Skevington – hence, by corruption, its popular name. The Scavenger's Daughter was conceived as the perfect complement to the Duke of Exeter's Daughter,

Stretched out on the Newgate floor, the heavy weights pressing down upon his chest, Thomas Spiggott continues obdurately to resist the pressure to plead. Defiant as he was, though, Spiggott would yield in the end: he too in time was successfully 'pressed to plead'.

the rack. Skeffington's gyves, as it was also known, worked in the opposite direction from the rack by compressing the body rather than stretching it. Essentially a hinged iron hoop in which the victim was made to kneel, hands tied behind his back, it was then locked shut from behind and tightened with a screw. As the Jesuit historian Mathew Tanner explained:

> [The torture] binds as in a ball, holding the body in a threefold manner, the lower legs being pressed to the thighs, the thighs into the belly and both are locked with two iron clamps ... pressed against each other and the body of the victim is almost broken by this compression ... more cruel than the rack ... the whole body is so bent that blood exudes from the tips of the hands and feet ... the box of the chest being burst and a quantity of blood is expelled from the mouth and nostrils.

The Scavenger's Daughter was an ingenious arrangement of wrought iron that brought to bear enough pressure to all but burst the body it constrained. It marked a macabre milestone in the history of torture technology.

The ideal instrument for the prisoner who had somehow succeeded in withstanding the pains of the rack, the Scavenger's Daughter appealed to torturers on account of its portability. Far too cumbersome ever to be moved, the rack might take pride of place in a centre of torture such as the Tower, but it could not be taken on the hunt for heresy and treason out in the provinces. Skeffington's gyves, on the other hand, could accompany the torturer the length and breadth of the land, and could even be quickly folded up and carried from room to room. This method was also preferred to the rack by those torturers sufficiently 'sensitive' to their female victims' modesty: They did not need to be stripped of their shifts to meet the Scavenger's Daughter.

Cruel minds do, as we have seen, tend to think alike, and Skeffington's invention finds an interesting parallel in the ancient Indian torture of *anundal*, which achieved much the same results by a system of ropes and cords. As George Ryley Scott records in his book *A History of Torture*, first published in 1940:

> *Anundal* consisted of compelling the victim to remain for a considerable length of time in a most unnatural or abnormal, and consequently painful,

position. The ingenuity of the executioner was given full play. The head of the prisoner would be forced down and tied to his feet by means of a rope or belt passed around his neck and under the toes. Or one leg would be forced upward to the uttermost extent and fastened to the neck, compelling the victim to stand in this agonizing position. Or the arms and legs, forcibly interlaced to the point almost of dislocation, were bound so as to be immovable. In other cases heavy stones were fastened to the victim's back, which was often stripped naked, the sharp edges cutting into the flesh. In each variety of punishment it frequently happened that the executioner would sit astride of the culprit's body at frequent intervals in order to increase the torment.

Versions of this form of rope restraint are still in use today. The most notorious is perhaps the method of 'five-point tying' used in many African countries. This involves the victim's back being arched backwards, every movement he makes in his struggles simply tightening the ropes around his ankles, wrists and neck. Other torturers prefer to pass one of the victim's hands back over his head and thrust the other up behind his back before tying the thumbs tightly together. The position is not only one of excruciating agony, but opens up the whole upper body for a thorough beating.

The court martial book for the British Army's Tangier Garrison for 1663–69 makes fascinating, if horrific, reading, and offers some insight into the wide range of appalling options open to dissatisfied superior offices before the Mutiny Act of 1689 imposed restrictions on them. Among the punishments meted out during this period was that given to a soldier found drunk at his post, who was sentenced to be 'tied neck and heels, with his head forced between his knees by two muskets, and kept there for an hour, till the blood gushed out of his nose, mouth and ears'.

The punishment of 'tying neck and heels' – a version of which was also used in interrogating suspects in the Massachusetts witch-hunts of the early 1690s – was taken up enthusiastically by Britain's Royal Navy in the 19th century. Like the Army, the Navy used muskets, forcing the offender to sit down on the deck with one weapon passed beneath his knees, and another across the back of his neck. These provided rigid transversals that could be pulled tightly together with leather straps to exert enormous pressure on the victim's body, forcing out blood from the mouth, nose and ears.

An early exploit of Davy Morgan, a career criminal eventually hanged for murder in 1712, illustrates how the criminal classes might

————

This involves the victim's back being arched backwards, every movement simply tightening the ropes around his ankles, wrists and necks

————

also appropriate such techniques. The deed was recounted many years later in the *Newgate Calendar*, circa 1773:

> After he had procured his liberty again he broke, one night, into the house of Doctor Titus Oates, in Axe Yard, in Westminster, and stood sentinel over that reverend divine whilst his comrades rifled most of the rooms; and then, tying him neck and heels, after the same manner as they do a soldier, with a couple of muskets which they found in the kitchen, Davy very sorely gagged him, saying that if his mouth had been as well crammed but a few years ago, he had not sworn so many men's lives away for pastime.

A catalogue of vices

Tortures like the Scavenger's Daughter and the *anundal* subject the victim's whole body to terrible pressure. The force of compression can be concentrated a good deal more closely than this, however, as it was by the Sri Lankan sergeant who, in June 1998, closed a drawer in his office desk hard on a Tamil suspect's testicles and held it shut. This sort of intensely localized pressure is key to the effectiveness of a long series of vice-like instruments of low-tech simplicity.

A set of thumbscrews has the unassuming look of some inoffensive household utensil

The opportunities for improvisation with such devices may appeal to the torturer's cruel creativity. It certainly seems to have done so for those Greek policemen who, in 1990, were reported to have placed ballpoint pens between the fingers of a Turkish Kurd before crushing them together. Similarly, in 1745, a Scottish official thought of removing a tooth from an agricultural harrow, inserting his suspect's finger into the resulting hole and then driving the iron tooth back in, alongside the finger.

Unlike these makeshift means of torture, the thumbscrew was purpose designed. Set next to the rack, with its awesome potential to induce fear, or even the grim, gothic mechanism of the Scavenger's Daughter, a set of thumbscrews has the unassuming look of some inoffensive household utensil. Yet it was equally horrific in effect. Effortlessly portable, it could be slipped easily into a pocket or purse; the ultimate in efficiency, it extracted the maximum of pain from the prisoner with the minimum of effort by the interrogator.

Not unlike a nutcracker in appearance, the thumbscrew consisted at its simplest of a couple of lengths of iron that closed gradually together when tightened with a wing-nut screw. While smaller thumbscrews had grooves for only one or two thumbs, more sophisticated, 'double-decker' versions could accommodate both thumbs and several fingers

A rack which, instead of stretching, squeezed (drawing ropes tight around the wrists and ankles), is shown in an 1824 edition of Foxe's Book of Martyrs. Foxe's openly propagandist book is not the most reliable guide, yet the rack seen here strikingly resembles other, better-documented examples.

simultaneously. Sharp studs inside might intensify the wearer's agony. Even without these refinements, the thumbscrew was quite capable of inflicting unbearable pain and fearsome injuries.

Crude thumbscrews, known as 'pilniewinkies' or 'pennywicks', were employed in Scotland in the 14th century – a late date, in fact, for what is widely assumed to have been an instrument of medieval torture. More

Thankfully no more than a simulation staged by Amnesty International for publicity purposes, this image still shows vividly how the victim can both literally and psychologically be tied up in knots by the clever torturer.

sophisticated thumbscrews do not seem to have been used until rather later, in 1660, when the Scots royalist Thomas 'Bluidy Tam' Dalyell was said to have brought back a set to Scotland on his return from exile in Russia after the Restoration of Charles II in England. Whether or not that story is actually true, the timing seems about right, as thumbscrews became most prevalent in Britain in the final decades of the 17th century.

In continental Europe, though, these devices seem to have been in use a good deal earlier, as had a related torture in which thumbs or fingers were squeezed in tightened loops of rope or cord. Named – with considerable and grim irony – the *sibille* in Italian, after the Sybil of classical mythology who guarded the Delphic Oracle and thus tended to the truth, this torture seems to have been applied in particular to women. In 1612, the 19-year-old Artemisia Gentileschi (not yet the world-famous painter she would one day become) was put to the test by *sibille* at the trial of her teacher Agostino Tassi. He was accused of sexually assaulting his young charge, and despite a dubious character that included a record of rape, the trial nevertheless came down to a question of his word against Artemisia's. She seems to have stood her torture bravely and secured a conviction against Agostino, who served time in prison as a result, though she may well have felt in retrospect that she had been punished more severely than her attacker.

This punishment would be used in Britain, too, especially later on, in the 18th century, when the old method of 'pressing to plead', though still legal, was becoming more controversial. Thus the torture of twisting the thumbs and fingers in whipcord began to be employed as an alternative or preliminary to the press. Not that it was necessarily such a 'light' torture: three cords in turn were snapped by the sheer force of the torture inflicted on Mary Andrews in 1721, before the fourth finally persuaded her to plead. Twenty years later, a judge at the Cambridge Assizes ordered an uncooperative prisoner to have his thumbs twisted in whipcord; when that failed to bring about the desired result, he was taken to the press, where a weight of 114kg (250lb) brought him round.

Cords and other armatures could also be tightened not only round the fingers, but around the forehead and temples, a torture used against nationalist agitators in the years leading up to Italian unification in the 1860s. The method was used much earlier than this, though. It was recorded in 1590, when the Scottish servant-girl Geillis Duncan fell under suspicion of witchcraft:

> Her maister, to the intent that he might the better trie and finde out the truth of the same, did with the help of others torment her with the torture of the Pilliwinkes upon her fingers, which is a grievous torture,

Three cords in turn were snapped by the sheer force of the torture inflicted on Mary Andrews

and binding or wrinching her head with a cord or roape, which is a most cruell torment also, yet she would not confess anie thing.

Another Scot, John Fiennes, found his head being 'thrawed with a rope' when, at the start of the 17th century, he was said to have raised, by sorcery, a storm which came close to sinking the ship carrying King James VI (James I of England) on his way to a royal visit to Denmark.

This method of torture had often been used in Germany since medieval times. There was even a mechanized version – a sort of enlarged thumbscrew fitted with a cap that was big enough to enclose the crown of the head. Once this had been tightened hard enough to dislodge the teeth from the victim's jaw, the pain could be intensified still further by the torturer rapping on the iron skull casing. The tiniest tap on the metal surface at this stage sent shockwaves pulsing down to the victim's very toes – the crowning pain of a particularly brutal torture.

As for the thumbscrews proper, it dropped out of official history during the 18th century, though as with so many tortures it continued to be used on the colonial slave plantations. The appearance, as recently as 1983, of thumbscrews in a list of categories of 'security equipment' requiring a special government licence for export from the United States suggests that there are parts of the world where this nasty little tool still has its uses.

The Spanish Jesuit missionary Alvarez Semedo, working in China in the early 17th century, saw a punishment not unlike a larger version of the thumbscrews being used. It is described in his History of China, from 1655:

The tiniest tap on the metal surface sent shockwaves pulsing down to the victim's very toes

For the feet they use an instrument called *kia quen*. It consisteth of three pieces of wood put in one traverse, that in the middle is fixt, the other two are moveable, between these the feet are put, where they are squeezed and prest, till the heel-bone run into the foot: for the hands they use also certain small pieces of wood between the fingers, they call them *tean zu*, then they straiten them very hard, and seale them round about with paper, and so they leave them for some space of time.

Sir George Staunton's distinguished study of the Penal Code of China (1810) elaborates a little on Semedo's description, explaining that these tortures tended to be employed particularly on those suspected of such serious crimes as robbery or murder; that the *kia quen* was reserved for men, and the *tean zu* for women. An Indian variant, the *kittee*, two wooden boards hinged at one end but screwed down just like its western

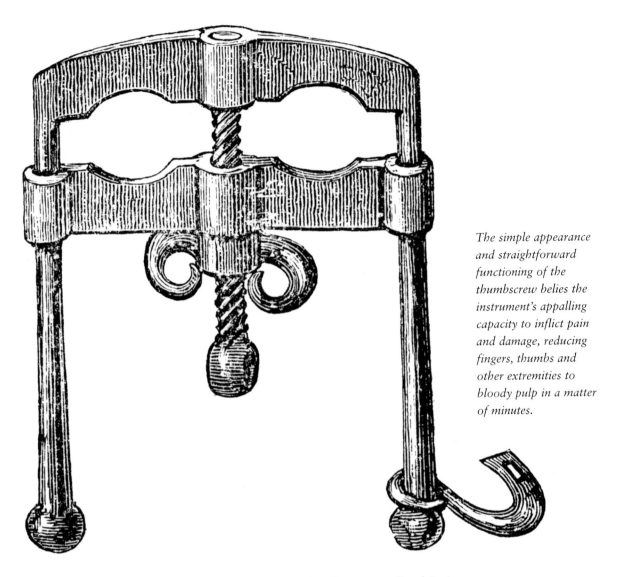

The simple appearance and straightforward functioning of the thumbscrew belies the instrument's appalling capacity to inflict pain and damage, reducing fingers, thumbs and other extremities to bloody pulp in a matter of minutes.

equivalent, was bigger than the thumbscrews but less specialized in its use, and could be applied to thumbs and fingers, hands and feet, ears and noses, nipples and genitals.

Torture has been a part of Indian life for centuries. In precolonial times, local rulers seem always to have used it, while under the British Raj, tax officials were allowed to employ it to exact what were regarded as their rightful revenues from an often reluctant peasantry. The *kittee* was the ideal instrument of torture for travelling excisemen: cheap, convenient, readily portable and above all effective. Where a heavier-

While one woman looks on from the comparative comfort of the stocks another has her hands crushed in a variant of the 'boot' in this understated scene from a sixteenth-century woodcut.

duty torture was wanted, two men could effectively be their own *kittee*, with the help of two thick rods of bamboo. Placing one on the floor, they would then lay their victim on his back across it; laying the other rod crossways across his chest, the torturers would then sit or stand with their full weight upon either end, moving the rod up the chest and down the abdomen to the legs as required. This torture is still widespread today, according to Physicians for Human Rights, who add that, even where the torture is restricted to the thighs, so that vital organs are apparently not affected, 'the release of toxins from damaged muscles … may cause acute renal (kidney) failure'.

Rather than being made to lie flat on the floor, Sikh suspects – who are bound by their religion never to cut their hair – are forced to sit upright for this torture: a third officer stands behind him, his knee thrust hard into his spine while he pulls back hard on his unravelled hair.

The iron boot

'Bloody Tam' Dalyell would have had ample opportunity for trying out his Muscovite thumbscrews: The Restoration of Stuart rule in Scotland meant a restoration of old intolerances. Presbyterian protestants who had supported Cromwell and his English Roundheads were rooted out wherever they hid and subjected to torture – using not only Tam's thumbscrews, but such antique methods as the 'boot'. Basically a boot made of iron, which encased both foot and lower leg, its means of operation was terrifyingly simple. The 19th-century novelist Sir Walter Scott describes this torture in his 1816 novel *Old Mortality*, in a fictional episode that must have owed all too much to harrowing fact:

> The executioner enclosed the leg and knee within the tight iron case, and then placing a wedge of the same metal between the knee and the edge of the machine, took a mallet in his hand and stood waiting for further orders. A surgeon placed himself by the other side of the prisoner's chair, bared the prisoner's arm, and applied his thumb to the pulse in order to regulate the torture according to the strength of the patient. When these preparations were made, the President glanced his eye around the Council as if to collect their suffrage, and judging from their mute signs, gave a nod to the executioner whose mallet instantly descended on the wedge, and forcing it between the knee and the iron boot, occasioned the most exquisite pain, as was evident from the flush on the brow and cheeks of the sufferer.

Scott's description, though atmospheric and correct in formal details, reflects only palely the realities of what one modern commentator has called 'the torture of the bone and marrow mixing Boot'. Iron or wooden wedges were driven in one at a time up to a number of eleven or more, each one lacerating the flesh and splintering the bone more horribly than the last. So hideous was the whole experience that an order had to be passed compelling council members to stay and watch it. So many fled from the mere prospect of being present that the proceedings against the accused threatened to collapse for want of witnesses. It goes without saying that few walked away from this torture – or indeed ever walked freely for the remainder of their lives.

The French brodequin was a derivative of the boot. Its name comes from the light shoe used as inner lining for a big military boot, though

Scott's description reflects only palely the realities of what one modern commentator has called 'the torture of the bone and marrow mixing Boot'

there was no real physical resemblance as there was with the Scottish boot. Rather, the *brodequin* encased the sufferer's legs in a wooden box, with a further pair of planks running down the middle to separate the knees. Tightly knotted cords held the victim still and formed an integral part of the torture. A series of wedges driven between these central planks pressed them further and further outwards, subjecting the prisoner's legs to the most enormous pressure and excruciating pain as the cords bit deep into flesh and bone.

More labour intensive than its European equivalent, this Chinese version of the brodequin *requires two men to hold the casing taut with ropes, while a third drives in the wedges with his hammer.*

Despite its French name and pedigree, the brodequin seems to have been used mostly in Scotland – as, for that matter, was the so-called 'Spanish Boot' or 'cashielaw'. (The Scots name is said to have come from the Old French *casse-loix*, meaning 'warm hose'.) Very similar to the old-fashioned Scottish boot in design, except that it was tightened not with wedges but by means of a screw, the cashielaw was simultaneously heated in a portable furnace. While a screw-driven boot

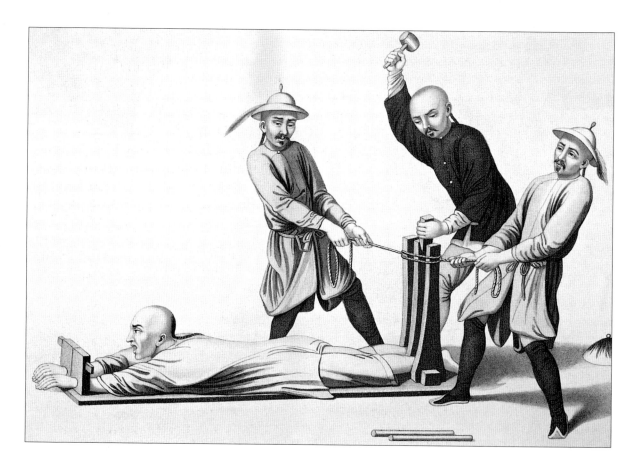

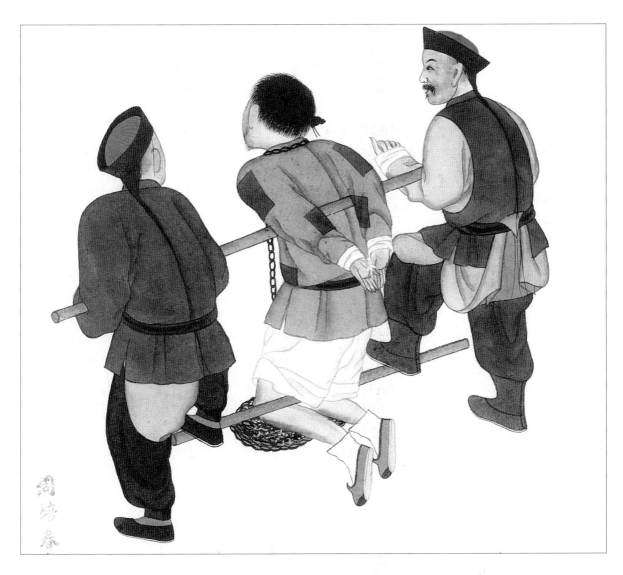

does indeed seem to have been used in Spain, that country's major contribution to this branch of torture technology seems to have been an oversized iron boot into which boiling water, oil or pitch were poured.

While this particular technique would have offered its own unique torments, the agonies wrought by the crudest form of boot or thumbscrew were no less severe. Certainly, it is a peculiarly dehumanising branch of torture that subjects the body to the forces of mechanical compression, or – in the case of the press – the most basic law of gravity.

In this Chinese variant of the Indian kittee, *from around 1900, the downward pressure of the rod behind the legs is rendered still more damaging by the victim being forced to kneel upon a jagged coil.*

Chapter Four

Trial by Fire

In what was normally a bustling city square, pandemonium reigned, such was the throng of people and the glare of lanterns and torches. Churches all around Valladolid's Plaza Mayor had been offering masses since the small hours. Onlookers crowded the rooftops, still silhouetted in the half-darkness of early morning. Curious eyes looked out from every window; every balcony bristled with sightseers – all eager for a view of the massive wooden stage where those accused of heresy stood, on this Feast of the Holy Trinity, 21 May 1559.

Chief among the 30 accused was the noted theologian Dr Cazalla. With him were eminent lawyers, respected priests and leading members of the local gentry and wealthy, mercantile classes. Dr Cazalla's crime had been to start a secret congregation of Lutheran worship in the city at a time when the Catholic Church and the Inquisition were in no mood to brook dissent in its Spanish bastion. Dr Cazalla pleaded for his own life and those of his sister Beatriz and his friends, but this did nothing to sway the decision of the court: he, most of all, had to be consigned to the flames. His repentance had brought him this much grace, however: he would be garrotted to death at the stake, rather than being eaten away, inch by agonizing inch, by the rising flames. Thirteen others who had joined him in expressing remorse for their heretical ways were granted similar leniency; only the lawyer Herrezuelo, who stood defiant, was to be burned alive – a disappointment to those spectators motivated by sheer sadism.

Yet the Holy Office would surely have been pleased at the extent to which it had managed to catch the imagination of every section of Spanish society. The message was loud and unambiguous: God was great, and the reach of His Inquisition was long. This was, of course, precisely what inquisitor General Fernando de Valdes had intended when he devised this new lavish ceremonial, *auto-da-fé*, meaning 'act of faith'. Previously, the work of the Inquisition had been conducted behind closed doors, but this elaborately conceived public rite was designed to unite its audience in equal measures of piety and terror. Valdes had succeeded in staging what amounted to nothing less than a spectacular theatrical enactment of the Last Judgment – at which time, according to Christian scripture, God will cast the wicked into the fires of eternal damnation.

Whatever ingenuities might be imagined, no tool of the torturer is more elementally terrifying than the naked flame. Here, in an 18th-century engraving, one can almost feel the fierce heat, smell the stench of seared flesh and hear the screams of suffering.

*The infernal
punishments meted out
to heretics after a
Spanish auto-da-fé are
vividly shown in this
18th-century Dutch
engraving. The 'Black
Legend' promoted by the
protestant powers
exaggerated the
atrocities of Catholic
Spain, yet there could
be no denying the
many cruelties of the
Inquisition.*

Tried by ordeal

Fire is not, of course, used by torturers simply on account of its theological symbolism, as those who have endured cigarette burns or drips of molten polythene in modern interrogations can testify. But if the pure pain of seared human flesh is acute, so too is the terror aroused by the menacing glow of fire itself, its elemental force and, in many traditions, its sacral power. Ordeal by fire has long had a profound resonance in many cultures. From those eastern mystics who walk unscathed over smouldering coals to the biblical prophets who were flung into furnaces but emerged untouched, there has been widespread religious belief that God will spare His own from the flames. From this follows on, all too easily, the idea that a defendant's guilt or innocence might be proved under pain of fire: those who have done no wrong, went the reasoning, would be kept from harm by divine intervention.

There are references to trial by fire in the writings of the Greek dramatist Sophocles in the 5th century BC, but it seems to have had its heyday in early-medieval Europe. It was only to be expected that fire – issuing straight from the volcanic smithies of the Underworld – would inevitably have a certain mystique for Nordic pagans. Yet its use in northern Europe actually appears to have begun comparatively late, under the auspices of Christianity, and it endured well into the medieval era, administered by the Church. Whatever its origins, by the end of the first millennium the ancient ritual had been cloaked in Christian liturgical formulae, as an early German document makes only too clear:

> After the accusation has been lawfully made … the priest … shall take with a tongs the iron placed before the altar; and, singing the hymn … he shall bear it to the fire, and shall say this prayer over the place where the fire is to carry out the judgment: 'Bless, O Lord God, this place, that there may be for us in it sanctity, chastity, virtue and victory, and sanctimony, humility, goodness, gentleness and plenitude of law, and obedience to God the Father and the Son and the Holy Ghost.' After this, the iron shall be placed in the fire and shall be sprinkled with holy water, and while it is heating, he shall celebrate mass … And straightway the accused shall carry the iron to a distance of nine feet. Finally his hand shall be covered under seal for three days, and if festering blood be found in the track of the iron, he shall be judged guilty. But if, however, he shall go forth uninjured, praise shall be rendered to God.

By the end of the First Millennium the ancient ritual had been cloaked in Christian liturgical formulae

The 13th-century legend of Queen Emma and her ordeal at Winchester Abbey, while almost certainly untrue, does serve to highlight another form of ordeal by fire. Emma or, in the original Anglo-Saxon, Oelfgifa, was the wife first of King Aethelred the Unraed and, after he died, of King Cnut the Great. Some years after her second husband's death, the dowager queen was suspected of having an affair with Aelfrine, Bishop of Winchester. She would, she announced, submit to ordeal to prove her innocence. The King and his bishops accordingly agreed that she would be put to the severest test – to walk with bare feet over nine red-hot ploughshares. The ploughshares were duly heated to glowing incandescence and laid carefully on the floor. Blindfolded Oelfgifa was led slowly across them. 'When will we reach the ploughshares?' she asked, as she stepped, uninjured, off the last one. On examination, the soles of her feet proved quite unblemished.

While there are serious reasons to doubt the veracity of this account, the ordeal of walking over red-hot iron bars or ploughshares is a matter of record. The bars might be spaced irregularly to confuse the blindfolded victim, or he or she might simply be forced to step upon each one. On occasion, 12 bars would be used instead of the standard nine. Trial by ordeal was traditionally measured out in multiples of three, the number of the Holy Trinity and a sacred number in Catholicism. Nine or 12 bars might be negotiated on the ground, or a single bar carried by hand for a distance of nine feet; the binding to be removed and the wound examined after three days.

Trial by water

Another trial popular in Europe at the same time was the ordeal by boiling water, which was similarly administered. Again, the punishment took place in a church under the supervision of a priest; in this case, however, the prisoner had to plunge his hand into a vessel of boiling water to retrieve a ring or coin or some other object. As with the ordeal by fire, there would be a long and elaborate preamble of prayer and fasting, and vessel and victim alike would be blessed with holy water. The injured arm would be bound with bandages, which were removed after three days. A prisoner emerging unscathed was deemed innocent. The use of this ordeal was not confined to Christendom, being recorded in India as late as the mid-19th century. In 1867, the *Bombay Gazette* reported the case of a camel driver forced to plunge his hand into boiling oil to dispel suspicions that he had committed theft. Tyrannical householders might also test the honour of wives or servants in this way. One Tanjore man is reported in 1846 to have plunged the hands

The medieval ordeal of boiling water, as imagined by a French engraver of the late 18th century, by which time such practices very much belonged to the sort of history of 'superstition' from which this illustration has been taken.

At Phalaris's court one man suffers strappado, *another is racked, while a third cooks in Perilaus's brazen bull.*

of three servants into boiling cow dung in an attempt to force a confession of theft.

Various theories have been offered to explain how injury might have been prevented during trial by ordeal. Voltaire suggested in the 18th century that victims might first have rubbed a mixture of vitriol spirit, alum and the juice of onions into the skin. There seems to be no modern scientific evidence to suggest that this would have helped in any way – or to support the claim that iron brought to 'white heat', rather than 'red', can be safely touched. Such attempts at explanation miss the mark completely: trial by ordeal could make sense only in an age of absolute faith – or, as we might say, superstition. To the modern sensibility the process can only seem cruelly perverse: leaving aside the dreadful pain to be endured by those who might yet be found innocent, the odds were stacked heavily against the defendant, since a blister 'half as large as a walnut' would suffice as evidence of his guilt. That anyone at all came through unscathed would seem remarkable. The fact that over the centuries a sizeable number appear to have done so suggests that officiating priests – whether motivated by Christian compassion or baser corruption – must have had a hand in rigging the proceedings.

In fact, by the late 12th century a less credulous age was coming to look askance at a system that had no basis in earthly justice. It is natural for burns to blister, and to expect them not to was effectively to ask for a miracle. Was it not blasphemy, asked the influential clerical critic Peter the Chanter to call on God to intervene in this way? In addition, concern had been growing throughout the century over the number of people condemned after trial by ordeal when all the ordinary, earthly evidence would appear to acquit them. In 1210, a watershed was reached when the Bishop of Strasbourg ordered a large group of heretics to be tried by ordeal. One of the condemned appealed against the bishop's judgment and Pope Innocent III upheld his plea, banning the ordeal altogether five years later.

Was it not blasphemy, asked Peter the Chanter, to call on God to intervene in this way?

Burning and boiling

The classical record is vague about trial by ordeal, but, thanks to the writing of the Roman satirist Lucian in the 2nd century BC, we have a comparatively detailed knowledge of that diabolical engine of torture, Perilaus's Brazen Bull. The inventor Perilaus constructed a life-sized bronze sculpture of a bull with a rear entrance providing access to its belly. Here, hapless victims were enclosed while a fire was lit beneath the creature's belly. By an elaborate system of pipes, cunningly contrived, the victim's screams issued from the bull's mouth in the form of a gentle lowing. Proudly presenting his invention to the Greek tyrant Phalaris, Perilaus was taken aback to find himself seized and put inside. No fitter end could there be for the deviser of such a diabolical instrument, said Phalaris.

Killed in a similar fashion was St Lawrence, in Rome in 258 AD. He was burned, tradition has it, on a gridiron. When the saint was done on one side, the story goes, he cheerfully announced the fact to his tormentors, suggesting that they might now wish to turn him over. They might even want to take a taste, he added, to see whether he was better raw or cooked. Though he was in fact almost certainly beheaded, the far more colourful gridiron story has persisted, earning Lawrence the longstanding title of Patron Saint of Cooks.

If Lawrence's martyrdom was a matter of heroic humour, then the application of everyday, domestic cooking techniques to human victims has been anything but amusing. The ancient historian Josephus records that the Jewish rebels against Roman rule, the Maccabees, were subjected on capture to the most appalling of tortures, culminating in either being boiled or fried to death. In both cases, the techniques involved were pretty much as they sound: the victim was plunged into a cauldron of boiling water, oil or tallow, or sauteed in boiling oil on a hot iron surface. Likewise, medieval inquisitors in Italy and Spain are said to have greased the feet of prisoners either seated in the stocks or held down by warders on the floor, and effectively fried them in the heat of a nearby fire. The 'iron chair' rationalized this torture. It was equipped with shackles to hold the victim down, as well as its own built-in brazier at the prisoner's feet, with perhaps another beneath the seat itself.

Sun-Tzu tells the story of an angry king who boiled his enemy's unfortunate emissary

The Chinese historian and military philosopher Sun-Tzu tells the story of an angry king who boiled his enemy's unfortunate emissary, while similar punishments are reported to have been inflicted frequently by the emperors of first-millennium Japan. Such stories, however, though quite possibly true, are hardly well documented. The evidence for this form of punishment being used in India at a later time is rather better. The Sikh martyr Bhai Dyala met his end this way in the religious persecutions of the 1670s.

Boiling was by no means confined to the Middle and Far East. Versions of the punishment survived late into the history of early-modern Europe; France only abolished death by boiling in 1791. In England, the punishment was introduced under the reign of Henry VIII to punish Richard Roose, a cook who had taken advantage of his post to poison 17 members of the Bishop of Rochester's household. A special Act of Parliament was passed, appointing a punishment to fit so heinous a crime. Roose, it was decreed, should be 'boyled to death withoute havynge any advauntage of clergie'. The law remained in place for 16 years, during which two maidservants were similarly punished for poisonings.

Death by boiling was not unknown before Henry's legislation. Indeed, it seems to have been the favoured punishment for those caught coining currency. *The Chronicle of the Grey Friars of London* reports how one unfortunate forger was suspended from a gantry by a chain and then lowered repeatedly into a vat of boiling water until he died. When the executioner at Tours, France, attempted to punish the coiner Loys Secretan in a like manner in 1488, the prisoner's bonds came adrift and he rose sputtering and screaming to the water's surface. Resisting the executioner's desperate attempts to push him back under, he was

Both bathed and showered in boiling oil, these victims' sufferings could, at least, hardly last very long, though the pain would have been excruciating.

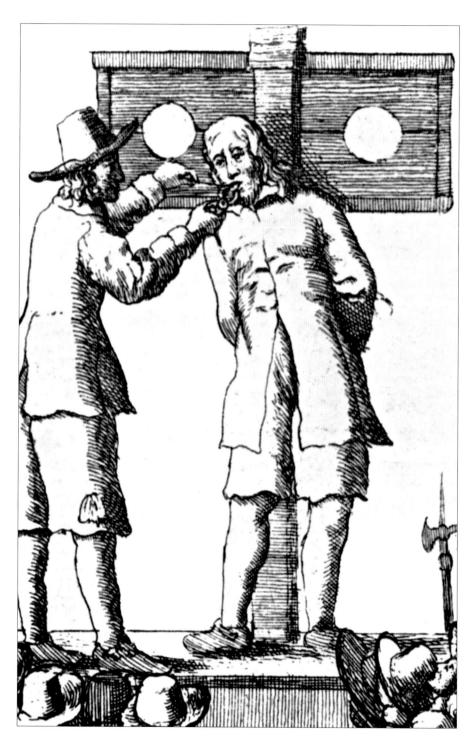

Convicted of blasphemy (which is to say, essentially, the expression of his Quaker beliefs) in 1656, James Nailor was sentenced to have his offending tongue bored through and was rendered speechless with a red hot iron. After this his forehead would be branded with a 'B' for 'blasphemer'.

eventually rescued by the watching mob, by now convinced that God had worked a miracle before their very eyes. Having saved the intended victim, the crowd fell furiously upon his would-be executioner, and ended up beating him to death in their pious frenzy.

Branded villains

Branding, a form of instant torture, and a lasting mark, is nowadays chiefly associated with animal livestock. The earliest known use of branding, in classical Roman times, was on runaway slaves who had been apprehended. With a large 'F' for *fugitivus* stamped on his brow, no runaway could realistically hope to get very far. Thieves, too, were often branded in ancient Rome. The pain and humiliation were part of the punishment, but there was a sense that it was in the public interest for light-fingered individuals to be clearly marked out to their fellow citizens. This practice was taken to its logical conclusion in the Britain of the Middle Ages, where a system of different letters was used to signify different crimes: an 'R' or 'V' for rogues or vagabonds; a 'T' for thieves; an 'M' for manslaughter; a 'P' for perjury; or an 'SL' for seditious libel. A fleur-de-lys sufficed for French offenders.

Though the earliest brandings were positioned discreetly at the base of the thumb (to draw attention to previous convictions when brought before the court), they later came to be placed more prominently on the cheek. Branding and mutilation tended to go together – those marked 'B' for blasphemer typically having to endure the further torture of having a red-hot skewer thrust through their sacrilegious tongues. In Scotland, where instead of a lettered iron a heated key was commonly used for brandings, miscreants were often also nailed by the ear to a public post for humiliation, or pierced through the earlobes with glowing irons.

Isabel Paterson of Cullen, who was caught stealing grain from a local farmer in 1636, was banished from the district on pain of branding. Paterson agreed that if she returned from her exile, she would be 'content to be taken and brunt with ane key upon the cheeke', before being banished again – this time on pain of death. Witnesses who saw Elspeth Rule being branded at Dumfries in 1701 would never forget her sufferings at the hands of an overzealous tormentor. They had, they swore, seen smoke pouring from her mouth. Another Scot, Alexander Leighton, a preacher, would encounter the brand not in his homeland but in the English capital of London. There, in 1628, deemed guilty of 'framing, publishing and dispersing a scandalous book directed against his King, peers and prelates', he was sentenced to a huge fine, pillorying and several whippings, branding (the letters 'SS', for 'sowing sedition',

Paterson agreed that if she returned from exile, she would be 'content to be taken and brunt with ane key upon the cheeke'

were placed on either side of his nose), the slitting of his nostrils, the removal of both ears and, finally, an everlasting term of imprisonment.

Britain did not abolish branding for civilians until 1829, although the practice had more or less fallen into disuse. It was still an official punishment in the armed forces, but in the form of tattooing. Pricking the skin relatively painlessly with needles, officers painted over the marks with a mixture of ink and gunpowder: 'D' for deserter, 'BC' for bad character and so on. The stigma was indelible, the punishment – before the whole regiment – humiliating, but this was not branding as it had been known before. France developed its own system of lettering ('TF' for *travaux forces*, or hard labour; 'T' for temps, or those simply serving time) and appeared to continue the practice of branding with red-hot metal until the end of the 18th century. In India, meanwhile, as recently as the 1990s, the Punjabi authorities had to pay compensation to four women who, having been convicted of pickpocketing, had the word 'thief' tattooed on their foreheads by members of the state police.

Burning at the stake

The most widespread form of death by fire, in Catholic and Protestant lands alike, was undoubtedly that of burning at the stake. The Spanish Inquisition of the 17th century may have elevated the practice to new heights of ritual pomp and circumstance, but this terrible punishment was already well established throughout Europe. Up until its demolition in 1874, the church of St Martin Outrich in London's Threadneedle Street was home to the grave of a certain Mrs Abigail Vaughan. This pious matron had lived in medieval times and distinguished herself in death by bequeathing in her will a sum of four shillings a year towards the cost of faggots for burning heretics.

This pious matron had bequeathed in her will a sum of four shillings a year towards the cost of faggots for burning heretics

The late 16th and early 17th centuries saw a literal witch-hunt that has been the model for all figurative ones ever since. For decades the rumours ran riot: tales of wild witches' Sabbats, of ritual cannibalism and the adoption of animal forms. Panic had a way of breeding panic, and soon the population was living in genuine fear. The Scottish city of Aberdeen seems to have been thrown into turmoil by the publication of King James VI's pamphlet, *Demonology*, in 1597. That year, no fewer than 23 suspected witches were burned at the stake, as well as one man, the son of a 'witch' who was believed to have joined in his mother's nefarious rituals.

England's most famous burnings at the stake were the work of another Catholic monarch, 'Bloody Mary'. One of her most celebrated victims was the sometime Archbishop of Canterbury, Thomas Cranmer, in 1556. Having refused to abjure his Anglican creed when the Queen re-established Catholicism on her accession in 1553, he had, under torture, at one point weakened sufficiently to sign a recantation of his views. Recovering his courage, however, he insisted again on his Protestantism, and was duly sentenced to be burned with the other Anglican martyrs. Asked for the last time to endorse his former recantation, he refused and, showing his hand, is reported to have said: 'This was the hand that wrote it, and therefore shall it suffer first punishment.'

One victim boils to death, while the other is consumed directly by the raging fire in this 18th-century engraving depicting the tortures of the ancient past.

'Fire being now put to him, he stretched out his right hand, and thrust it into the flame, and held it there a good space, before the fire came to any other part of his body; where his hand was seen of every man sensibly burning, crying with a loud voice, "This hand hath offended." As soon as the fire got up, he was very soon dead, never stirring or crying all the while.'

Though most victims were strangled at the stake before burning, as the law required, many do seem to have been deliberately burned alive. One of these was Prudence Lee, who was burned at Smithfield, London, in

1652, for the murder of her husband. As a pamphlet of the day reports:

> Then the executioners, setting her in a pitch barrel, bound her to the stake and placed the straw and faggots about her, whereupon she, lifting her eyes to Heaven, desired all present to pray for her. The executioner then putting the fire to the straw, she cried out 'Lord Jesus have mercy on my soul' and when the fire was kindled was heard to shriek out terribly some five or six several times.

The smallest of mercies

Even when an executioner was inclined to be merciful, his incompetence could render his good intentions irrelevant, as happened in the case of Catherine Hayes in 1726. She had been taken to the stake at London's Tyburn, and was in the process of being strangled to death in the officially approved style when the executioner burned his hands and recoiled, leaving his victim alive and in agony. It took her half an hour to die, the watching multitude apparently listening, unsympathetically, to the woman's screams. In the end, though, the attitude of executioner and crowd could make little difference to the outcome of a burning – the only thing that might was the outlook of the authorities, though they do not generally seem to have been distinguished by their compassion.

This was demonstrated tragically in the case of three Guernsey women, Kathleen Cawches and her two daughters, the youngest of whom was heavily pregnant, who in 1556 were sentenced to be burned at the stake for heresy. Though the executioner attempted to strangle them with a length of rope before the flames took hold, he was not quick enough; the rope caught fire and burned away before he could kill the victims. All three women burned alive, the youngest daughter in her death throes giving birth to a baby which was snatched from the flames by onlookers and handed to the officiating clergy. 'There was some deliberation by the priests', we are told, 'the Dean and the Bailiffs, the Provost and the island's Jurats, after which the Provost ordered the infant to be cast on the fire as an heretick.'

All four elements – Earth, Air, Fire and Water – have been mythologized throughout human history. And perhaps ordeal, and death, by fire on Earth could, according to the prevailing beliefs of the day, be legitimately sanctioned as having a genuine, spiritual – and purgative – correspondence with the flames of divine judgement. A more secular line of reasoning would doubtless conclude, as the first primitive ever to thrust a hand into naked flame surely discovered: the pain it inflicts is unimaginable. With such pain comes fear, that incomparable mechanism of state control.

Even when an executioner was inclined to be merciful, his incompetence could render his good intentions irrelevant

Chapter Five

Water Torture

Though the terrors of fire are obvious to behold, even from a distance, the potential for cruelty and suffering that lurks in the lifegiving force of water is no less devastating. The slowly maddening drip, drip, drip of the 'water torture' is notorious – the finest dribble directed to a single spot on the flesh is said to be excruciating. Torturers have valued water chiefly, though, as a means of drowning. The partial suffocation that occurs when the head is immersed in water will fill a victim with helpless panic. Other tortures may be more painful, but few are as demoralizing as this.

As modern torturers have found, a plastic bag slipped over the head brings the prisoner to the brink of suffocation in seconds. By way of refinement, the airtight bag can contain some chilli powder, cement dust or a drop of fuming petrol – a technique known as the 'dry *submarino*'. In the true *submarino* (the word comes from Spanish-speaking Latin America), the victim's head is simply thrust into a bucket of water and held there. Urine and faeces, vomit, detergent and other contaminants are often added to make the mixture that much more potent. A crude technique, to be sure, and yet the effectiveness of the *submarino*, wet or dry cannot be doubted. The prisoner who, marshalling all his resources, has been able to withstand more straightforward applications of pain, may well find his discipline deserting him when he reaches the point of drowning. The long-term complications associated with this sort of asphyxiation include everything from nosebleeds to respiratory problems both acute and chronic, and even – when dirty liquid has been breathed into the lungs – fatal pneumonia. From the torturer's point of view, however, no marks are left, and the victim recovers rapidly for further interrogation.

Drinking by force

When the Inquisition in Málaga tied William Lithgow to the rack in 1620, he would soon discover that the agonies offered by the contraption itself were not to be the worst of his sufferings:

> Then the tormenter … went to an earthen jar standing full of water, a little beneath my head: from whence carrying a pot full of water, in the bottom whereof was an incised hole, which being stopped by his thumb,

In a scene from the ferocious battle for the Philippines, as witnessed by a French observer in 1902, American troops torture a native official who has refused to reveal to them the whereabouts of the rebel forces.

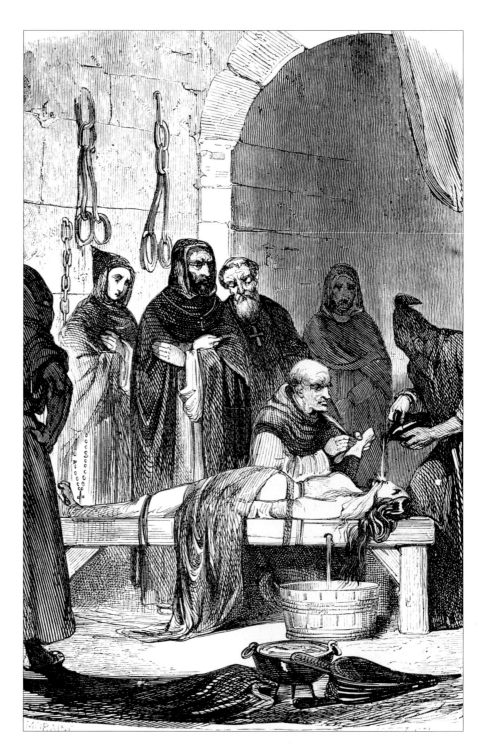

*Witnesses stand around
in attitudes of prayerful
piety and a secretary
takes scrupulous notes
as a cowled executioner
of the Inquisition puts
a woman to the water
torture. Note the
self-draining bench
on which the victim is
tied down, evidently
designed with this very
purpose in mind.*

till it came to my mouth, he did pour it in my belly ... the first and second devices I gladly received, such was the scorching drought of my tormenting pain, and likewise I had drunk none for three days before. But afterward, at the third charge perceiving these measures of water to be inflicted upon me as tortures, O strangling tortures! I closed my lips again-standing that eager crudelity. Whereat the Alcaide enraged, set my teeth asunder with a pair of iron cadges, detaining them there, at every several turn, both mainly and manually; whereupon my hunger-clunged belly waxing great, grew drum-like imbolstred, for it being a suffocating pain, in regard of my head hanging downward, and the water reingorging itself, in my throat, with a struggling force, it strangled and swallowed up my breath from yowling and groaning.

Two years later Englishman John Clarke was tortured by the authorities in the Dutch East Indies by what would appear to have been a more sophisticated version of Lithgow's treatment:

First they hoisted him up by the hands with a cord on a large door ... Then they bound a cloth about his necke and face so close that little or no water could go by. That done, they poured the water softly upon his head untill the cloth was full, up to the mouth and nostrills, and somewhat higher; so that he could not draw breath, but he must withall suck in the water: which being still continued to be poured in softly, forced all his inward parts, came out of his nose, eares, and eyes, and often as it were stifling and choaking him, at length took away his breath, and brought him to a swounce or fainting. Then they tooke him quickly down, and made him vomit up the water. Being a little recovered, they triced him up againe, poured in the water as before, eftsoones taking him downe as he seemed to be stifled. In this manner they handled him three or four severall times with water, till his body was swolne twice or thrice as bigge as before, his cheekes like great bladders, and his eyes staring and strutting out beyond his forehead.

In Clarke's case a mass of cloth was clearly piled up around the face to act as a sort of funnel. Far more common, though, was the simple square of gauze described by the 17th-century Dutch chronicler Ernestus Eremundus Frisius:

The torturer throws over his [the victim's] mouth and nostrils a thin cloath, so that he is scarcely able to breathe thro' them, and in the mean while a small stream of water like a thread, not drop by drop, falls from

'The water reingorging itself, in my throat, it strangled and swallowed up my breath from yowling and groaning'

on high, upon the mouth of the person lying in this miserable condition, and so easily sinks down the thin cloth to the bottom of his throat, so that there is no possibility of breathing, his mouth being stopped with water and his nostrils with the cloth, so that the poor wretch is in the same agony as persons ready to die, and breathing out their last. When this cloth is drawn out of his throat, as it often is, so that he may answer to the questions, it is all wet with water and blood, and is like pulling his bowels through his mouth.

Though the name [chiffon] may hint at Parisian luxury, that impression could hardly be less appropriate

The use of the soft cloth gag is the basis for the torture of the chiffon used by Algerian torturers today, an enduring legacy of French colonial times. Though the name may hint at Parisian luxury, that impression could hardly be less appropriate. This form of torture generally involves cramming a rag, often impregnated with corrosive detergent, into the prisoner's mouth and forcing filthy water through it before the guards stamp on their victim's distended stomach so that the liquid comes spewing out again. Suspects under interrogation in Mexican police stations have been terrified to find themselves being held down, their heads tilted back and fizzy drinks forced up their nostrils. They feel as though their brains are exploding. A mixture of hot peppers might even be added to make the effect more potent.

Sink or swim

Water has been used throughout history as a supposed test of innocence. The witches of Aberdeen who met their death by fire in 1597 had first been subjected to the testimony of water. 'There was many of them', we are told, 'tried by swimming in the water, by binding of their two thumbs and their great toes together; for being thus cast in the water, they floated always above.' The practice of 'swimming a witch', or the 'cold-water ordeal' was a highly popular form of trial in Britain and Europe, though its roots stretch back to the dawn of Indo-European civilization. Four thousand years ago, the *Babylonian Code of Hammurabi* was prescribing the following test for an unproven charge of sorcery:

> If a man has laid a charge of witchcraft and has not justified it, he upon whom the witchcraft is laid shall go to the holy river; he shall plunge into the holy river and if the holy river overcome him, he who accused him shall take to himself his house.

The thinking behind the trial – also used for those accused of adultery – was that the river would spare the innocent and drown the

A Swedish crowd put a suspected witch to the test by 'drowning' in this 19th-century impression of a scene from the 17th century. If the water 'accepted' her and she sank, she was – if onlookers were quick enough – hauled to safety. If she was rejected, and floated, she would be burned.

A 19th-century artist's impression of a medieval trial by ordeal, the bound victim being thrown into consecrated water. The technique of 'drowning' would, by the early-modern period, have become associated exclusively with finding witches: previously, though, it had been far more general in its application.

guilty. Under the Assyrians, however, the rules came to be reversed. Now it was the guilty, rejected by the river, who floated and the guiltless who began to sink – but who would, in theory at least, be dragged to safety once their innocence was established by the attendant witnesses. It is in this form that the trial came to medieval Europe, and, like the ordeals of fire and boiling water, took on the mantle of Christian rhetoric and ritual. The priest charged with undertaking the ritual would first address the accused in terms more or less like those given here, from a German example:

> May omnipotent God, who did order baptism to be made by water, and did grant remission of sins to men through baptism: may He, through His mercy, decree a right judgment through that water. If, namely, thou art guilty in that matter, may the water which received thee in baptism not receive thee now; if, however, thou art innocent, may the water which received thee in baptism receive thee now. Through Christ our Lord.

'If thou art innocent, may the water which received thee in baptism receive thee now'

Then, turning to face the pool or river appointed for the conduct of the ordeal, he would address the water, demanding that it should uphold its duty to see justice done. The prisoner would be stripped bare, bound hand and foot and then tied round with a length of knotted rope, the knot being positioned some distance from his body. He was then thrown into the water. If he sank far enough for the knot in the rope to be drawn beneath the surface, he was deemed innocent, and promptly pulled up again to safety. That, at least, was the theory. Yet many must have drowned in the process of establishing their innocence, while it would have been remarkably easy for malicious witnesses to hold up bodies that would have been inclined to float by their natural buoyancy. But trials by ordeal were never concerned with what we would today consider the most elementary basics of 'scientific evidence'. Early-medieval Christians were still in the habit of expecting miracles.

More surprising is the extent to which such superstitions endured into the early-modern era. Indeed, they found a new lease of life in the self-conscious, forward-looking cultures of Protestant northern Europe. The notorious 17th-century Suffolk witch-finder, Matthew Hopkins, on defending the charge that 'swimming' was no more than a savage torture, invoked not only royal authority and theological precedent, but also a sort of scientific justification for the practice:

> King James in his Demonology saith, it is a certaine rule for (saith he)
> Witches deny their baptisme when they Covenant with the Devill, water

being the sole element thereof, and therefore saith he, when they be heaved into the water, the water refuseth to receive them into her bosome, (they being such Miscreants to deny their baptisme) and suffers them to float, as the Froath on the Sea, which the water will not receive, but casts it up and downe, till it comes to the earthy element the shore, and there leaves it to consume.

Despite Hopkins' sanction of the ordeal, a certain uneasiness can be inferred from his insistence that, for all the admirable virtues of the test, 'It was never brought in against any [witches] at their tryals as any evidence.' There was outright opposition to the practice by humanitarian campaigners like Thomas Ady, whose 1656 treatise *A Candle in the Dark* questioned both the biblical basis and physical practicality of the cold-water ordeal as a trial for witchcraft.

Many in official circles were clearly uncomfortable with the whole institution of witch-swimming, but it was far too popular with the people to be banned. However, as time went on and the Age of Enlightenment dawned, the practice became increasingly untenable. Its last official use in England was in Leicester in 1717, when the court was told that the defendants, a mother and daughter, 'swam like a cork, a piece of paper, or an empty barrel, though they strove all they could to sink.' By that time the Lord Chief Justice, Lord Parker, had already made clear his severe disapproval of the practice, warning that:

'Witches deny their baptisme when they Covenant with the Devill, water being the sole element thereof'

> If any dare for the future to make use of that experiment, and the party lose her life by it, all they that were cause of it are guilty of willful murder ... neither King James' book nor all other precedents will save them from an halter.

His ruling held good for the ringleader of the mob that in 1751 lynched an elderly couple in Longmarston, Hertfordshire after a swimming, yet the case underlines how the tradition remained alive in the popular consciousness.

The ducking-stool

Tourist offices up and down Britain (and even in the picturesque towns of Britain's old colonies in the United States) point visitors to the sites where nagging women were ducked. The ducking-stool of 'Merrie England' is one of those tortures that has assumed a character of quaint curiosity, yet, while seldom actually fatal, the experience would hardly have seemed so trivial to its victims.

A *French* Dictionary of Superstitions *(1783) is the source for this image of a medieval ordeal by water. Enlightenment thinkers delighted in denouncing the absurd ideas and customs of the priest-ridden past: there is no evidence that these trials were really conducted so publicly or on anything like so large a scale.*

The theory that the ducking-stool was descended from the cuck- (or cack-) stool, which was in its turn derived ultimately from the commode, finds some support in the form of this ducking-stool from Sandwich, Kent.

Like the branks, or scold's bridle, which would in time replace it, the ducking-stool was a punishment reserved first and foremost for scolds, whose public punishment was considered an effective way of keeping women in line. Its predecessor was the 'cuckstool', a similar-sounding punishment that was, in fact, quite different. The name derives, some scholars say, from 'cack' (meaning excrement), because a commode was originally used in order to provide the utmost humiliation. The cuckstool was, therefore, primarily a means of punishment by shame, similar in function to the stocks and pillory. Sometimes, the victim might simply be set up before her own front door for general ridicule; at other times, her seat might be mounted on a wheeled 'tumbrell' and paraded through the streets to derisive jeers . And though the label of 'scold' seems to have been reserved overwhelmingly for women, the bylaws for Leicester in the 13th century show that men, too, might be subjected to this treatment:

> Alle maner scholdys that are dwellyng withinne this town, man or woman, that are founde defectyf by sworne men before the Miaer presented … to ponyssh them on a cukstool afore there dore as long as hym liketh and thanne so to be caried forth to the gates of the town.

There is no evidence that the 'cuckstool' was ever used for ducking, but the idea of such punishment had obviously occurred, hence the reference in the Domesday Book of 1084 to the 'chair' in Chester 'in which scolding women are to be seated and immersed in water'. Though there were considerable variations in what was always a locally administered punishment, the ducking-stool, as it developed through the Middle Ages consisted of a seat either mounted on or suspended underneath one end of a long, pivoted beam. The victim's tormentors controlled the other end of the beam. A wheeled platform meant the whole contraption could be put away or taken out of storage with ease – and, of course, it allowed its victims to be paraded in shame through the streets, just as with the cuckstool of old.

The device was designed pretty much along the lines of a harbour crane of the time, and indeed one such crane was used for the ducking punishment in Aberdeen in the 17th century. But few victims could hope for the comparatively hygienic immersion afforded by a seagoing dock. Most of these unfortunates were invariably ducked in the muddiest, most polluted stretches of water their persecutors could find. In 14th-century Hull, the 'cucking-pit' adjoined the ancient sewer, and victims came up from their duckings covered in excrement. How scrupulously such punishments were administered inevitably varied a good deal from place to place. The quarter sessions at Wakefield in 1692 was sufficiently humane to issue the following warning to two likely candidates for ducking:

But few victims could have hoped for the comparatively hygienic immersion afforded by a seagoing dock

> fforeasmuchas Katherine Hall and Margaret Robinson ... are grete disturbeours and disquieters of thier neighbours ... by reason of their daily scoldings and chydering the one with the other For The Reformacyon thereof ytt ys ORDERED that yf they doe hereafter contynue ... thenne JOHN MAWDE the high Constable ... shall cause theym to bee soundly ducked or cucked on the cuckstoole ...

If the shrewish shoemaker's wife Jane Farrett had received any warning she had not heeded it. In 1671 she had been ordered by the sessions to submit to three full duckings, 'over the head and ears'. At Neath, in Glamorgan, the stool could offer a careful gradation of punishment, since only when a certain 'pynn' was removed did it tip its victim down into the water. According to a local law of 1542:

> If any woman doe scolde or rage any Burgess or hys Wyfe or anie other Person and hys Wyfe, IF SHE BE found faultie in the same by six men, then shee to be brought at the first defaulte to the Cooking-Stoole and there to sitt one houre; at the seconde defaulte twoe houres and at the thirde defaulte to let slipp the pynn or else pay a good fyne to the Kynge.

Those who operated the ducking-stool at Warwick were free 'to plunge the woman into the water as often as it takes to cool her immoderate heat', but things could and did on occasion get out of hand. In 1731, a Nottingham woman drowned after having been 'duckt too muche and severely', and the mayor was subsequently prosecuted for his negligence in failing to protect her better. The trouble was that, given the public nature of the punishment, the ducking-stool was always liable to be, first and foremost, an instrument of mob justice. Magistrates might order its use, but once they had given the word they could not easily control the conduct of the punishment. Though constables and other officers of the law would have been present, the initiative, once things got going, lay with a boisterous and, very likely, drunken crowd. Part of the problem may have been that the authorities were already coming to see the ducking-stool as a useful means of keeping the populace amused, rather than a serious instrument of penal sanction.

It is tempting to speculate that even several centuries ago the ducking-stool had become part of local 'heritage'. Some places certainly appear to have been far prouder of their traditions in this regard than others. Duckings in the river by the bridge at Kingston-upon-Thames were already considered a venerable institution when on 19 August 1572 proceedings were taken against the 'wyffe to Downing, grave

'Plunge the woman into the water as often as it takes to cool her immoderate heat'

The jarring interruption to an idyllic rural scene, the gaunt crane-arm of the local ducking-stool cuts across our view of a quiet reach of the River Stour at Fordwich, near Canterbury, Kent.

Disloyal servants in medieval Norway, in this illustration from a 16th-century history, are punished by being drenched in icy water.

maker of this Paryshe'. She was 'sett on a newe cucking stoole made of gret hythe and so browght a bowte the markett place to Temes brydge And ther hadd iii [3] Duckynges over hed and eres because she was a common scolde and fyghter.' By 1745 when the landlady of the nearby pub, the Queen's Head, was ducked, she was watched by an audience of some 3000. If ducking was viewed first and foremost as a deterrent to bad behaviour, then it was singularly ineffective, as a report from the Kingston local paper, seven years earlier, makes clear:

> An elderly woman, notorious for her vociferation, was indicted for a common scold, and the facts alleged being fully proved, she was sentenced to receive the old punishment of being ducked, which was accordingly executed upon her in the Thames by the proper officers, in a chair for that purpose preserved in the town; and to prove the justice of the court's sentence upon her, on her return from the water-side she fell upon one of her acquaintance, without provocation, with tongue, tooth and nail, and would, had not the officers interposed have deserved a second punishment, even before she was dry from the first.

There were a number of ducking-stools scattered about central London. On 6 August 1611, Maudlin Tichon of St Martin's parish, having

> misbehaved herself in Scoulding and Abusing of her Neighbours with moste reproachful Speeches ... it was Ordered ... that according to the antient Custom of the Citty she should be fastened to a Boats Tayle and so be drawne through the Water to the other Side of the Thames ... this afternoon ...

The capital led the way in tiring of this custom, and by the end of the 17th century there are clear signs that it was dying out. Provincial England was far slower on the uptake. In Liverpool the custom even survived the rationalizations of the 18th century. A ducking-stool was rigged up beside a large bath in the central courtyard of the prison, and each new female inmate was ducked three times as a kind of initiation.

Cold showers

Sanitation has consistently been a problem for prison management, but cruel regimes have always been able to find cold water with which to torment their victims. Inmates at Birmingham Prison in the middle of the 19th century were stripped of their clothes and doused in icy water as punishment for the most minor transgressions of the rules. Long known as a recipe for quelling rebellious passions, the 'cold shower' as used in 19th-century prisons in the United States was a particularly brutal way of keeping prisoners in their place. A protracted spell in the regular showers under a constant jet of cold water could, and on occasion did, lead to death from hypothermia, but that was not

The 'cold shower' as used in the United States was a particularly brutal way of keeping prisoners in their place

The cleansing waters and the shocking pain of an enforced spell under a cold shower would both have been felt to play their part in the 'purification' of this habitual liar punished in Japan in 1904.

generally what the term 'cold shower' meant. It actually referred to the firing of a jet of ice-cold water from a high-pressure hose at a prisoner who had been previously strapped naked to a ladder. Both techniques were banned in US prisons in 1882, but the hosing of defenceless prisoners is still popular with torturers today in other parts of the world.

Survivors of torture in Turkey and Algeria have borne witness to the use of the pressure-hose there, while testimony from Chinese labour camps describes men and women being forced to stand naked in prison yards, in temperatures well below zero, while bucket after bucket of icy water was thrown over them. More recently, from Kurdistan come reports of one particularly vile water torture reserved by Turkish policemen for female suspects: They are immersed in a bath of cold water, while officers urinate into the bath around them; further testament to humanity's boundless imagination in the arena of cruelty.

The ultimate ordeal by water is, of course, the experience of drowning. Here, in what is presumably a mythological scene from landlocked Turkestan, in Central Asia, a condemned man must wait in suspense as, slowly but surely, the tide advances.

Chapter Six
Forces of Nature

The Greek hero Theseus had already tackled another cruel giant before he killed Procrustes on his rack-like bed (see Chapter Two). The bloodthirsty Sinis would seize unwary travellers, tying them between the bent-over trunks of adjacent pine trees. Once the trunks were released, they snapped back into position, tearing the suspended victims clean down the middle, from shoulders to groin. In the real world, despite their taste for hi-tech methods – as evidenced by everything from rack and thumbscrews to electric shocks – torturers have never been slow to harness the brute force of nature.

The grisly torture employed by Sinis is echoed in the medieval French epic, the *Song of Roland*, which details the punishment of Ganelon, the once-beloved knight who had betrayed his Lord Roland, his country and his Christian faith to the Saracen enemy, thereby allowing Muslim invaders into Spain. His pleas for mercy contemptuously spurned, he was tied by his wrists and ankles, then each extremity was roped to the pommel on the saddle of a bucking stallion. Four grooms leapt into their saddles and rode off at a gallop in different directions. The traitor was thus, quite literally, torn limb from limb. This punishment may, of course, have been every bit as mythical as that meted out by Sinis – yet torture in fact has always had a way of following torture in fiction.

When, in 1781, in Spanish-ruled Peru, the dangerous rebellion led by Jose Gabriel Condorcanqui was finally put down after months of bitter fighting, the question of how the leader was to be dealt with inevitably arose. Half-Spanish, half-Indian by blood, Condorcanqui was descended from the old Inca ruling family on his native side: and, as such, he had up to then been allowed the status of puppet ruler by the colonial authorities. His bid to win real freedom for his country was accordingly seen as a betrayal of the bitterest kind. The governor ordered that he be torn apart by horses – just like Ganelon. A much more recent version of this punishment is to be found in testimony taken from an inmate of the Omarska camp in Bosnia, where young Muslim men were held prisoner by the Serbs between 1992 and 1993:

The witness stated that a young Muslim man from Kozarac who had owned a Suzuki motorcycle was tortured in front of the other prisoners. He was severely beaten all over his body and his teeth were knocked out.

'Civilized' man has always set himself apart from Nature: the idea that he might form just another level on the food chain seems degrading to him – hence the humiliation of these Persian thieves hung out to be eaten by vultures.

The guards then tied one end of a wire tightly around his testicles and tied the other end to the victim's motorcycle. A guard got on the motorcycle and sped off.

The prejudices of the Crusaders lived on well into the Renaisssance, the Muslim Turks being regarded as little better than animals themselves. Here, in a woodcut made around 1500, a fittingly bestial form of torture is depicted: a Turk dragging a Christian captive behind his galloping horse.

In the early 1900s, the Mexican dictator Porfirio Diaz was ruthless in suppressing all forms of dissent, particularly from native Yaqui rebels, and his rural police officers, the Rurales – little more than a bunch of brigands with official badges – was happy to oblige. They are reported to have buried their captives up to the neck and trampled them beneath their horses' galloping hooves. Another punishment harnessing the power of the horse was that meted out in the mid-17th century by the Polish King Casimir to the handsome young Cossack leader, Ivan Stepanovich Mazeppa, after he was found to have had a liaison with Theresia, the beautiful young wife of a Polish count. The king had the Cossack bound hand and foot, then tied to the back of a wild stallion, which was then sent thundering across the endless steppe. In Byron's famous poem 'Mazeppa', written in 1819, the horse eventually collapses and Mazeppa manages to free himself and crawl to safety.

Horses are not the only animals to be have been used in torture. In India the traditional draught animal is the elephant. In 1814, a Bombay newspaper published this account of an execution in Baroda:

The man was a slave, and two days before had murdered his master, brother to a native chieftain, named Ameer Sahib. About 11 a.m. the elephant was brought out, with only the driver on his back, surrounded by natives with bamboo in their hands. The criminal was placed three yards behind on the ground, his legs tied by three ropes, which were fastened to a ring on the right hind leg of the animal. At every step the elephant took, it jerked him forwards, and eight or 10 steps must have dislocated every limb, for they were loose and broken when the elephant had proceeded 500 yards. The man, though covered with mud, showed every sign of life, and seemed to be in the most excruciating torments. After having been tortured in this manner about an hour, he was taken to the outside of the town, when the elephant, which is instructed for such purposes, is backed, and puts his foot on the head of the criminal.

Battle of the beasts

Four bas-reliefs from the tomb of Scaurus at Pompeii, dating from the middle of the 1st century BC, bring to life the Romans' own particular version of animal-related torture. The first of the Pompeiian combats shows the odds stacked heavily against a naked unarmed man, twisting and turning as he tries to evade attack by a lion and a panther. In the second scene, another unarmed victim attempts to dodge a charging wild boar. Should he escape the boar, a ferocious wolf lies in wait – his probable fate given graphic representation in a tableau to his right depicting a stag being torn apart by dogs or wolves.

The bestiarii set in combat against beasts might be condemned criminals (or, later, Christians); alternatively, they might be skilled professionals, working for pay. That would appear to be the case in the next Pompeiian scene, in which a semi-armoured man wields a spear against a pair of approaching animals. Though urged on from behind by an attendant with a goad, the bull and panther pitted against the bestiarius are chained together. According to archaeologists, this implies a training session rather than a fight to the death in the open arena, though by any standards the situation is a dangerous one. The fourth relief shows what appears to be a Spanish bullfighter, holding a sword in one hand, a dangling cape in the other. This was an accomplished matador, not a hapless victim – surely the bull had more to fear than he did.

'The man, though covered with mud, showed every sign of life, and seemed to be in the most excruciating torments'

Anyone participating in the games mounted in 186 BC might have been forgiven for worrying more about his own than the animals' welfare. Lions and panthers both featured here, though on nothing like the scale of later venationes, or 'hunts', such as that staged by the Cornelius Scipio Nasica and Lentulus in 168 BC. These games offered no fewer than 63 leopards and 40 bears, all of them tethered on long leashes, a precaution that struck later generations of Romans as unnecessarily tame. The games staged by Sulla involved 100 lions set free to hunt and be hunted in their turn by a troop of javelineers.

A growing taste for novelty is evident in the appearance of a hippopotamus and five crocodiles at Scaurus's games in 58 BC, They were housed in a little canal dug specially in the floor of the arena. The games given by Pompey in 55 BC boasted 600 lions and a battle between a troop of dart-throwing Gaetulians and 18–20 elephants. This encounter proved memorable for all the wrong reasons when, attempting to escape their persecution, the terrified beasts tried to climb the railings round the arena and seek safety on the terraces with the watching crowd. The event seems to have softened the hearts of the normally implacable spectators.

A growing taste for novelty is evident in the appearance of a hippopotamus and five crocodiles at Scaurus's games in 58 BC

However, such episodes did nothing in the long term to reduce the popularity of the games, which continued unabated into the first millennium AD. At the opening celebrations of the Colosseum in Rome, no fewer than 9000 wild animals were slaughtered over 100 days. (It is not reported how many bestiarii died in the course of this appalling carnage.) The Roman taste for 'bread and circuses' is of course well known, and successive rulers vied with one another to mount the goriest and the most spectacular of displays. Hence the shipwreck staged in the arena by Septimius Severus: lions, leopards, bison, wild asses and ostriches came spilling from the belly of the stricken vessel. At another event not long after, a vast model whale opened its mouth and a throng of 50 bears rushed out to meet the bestiarii's swords and spears.

The belief that the sand of the Colosseum's arena was saturated in the blood of Christians thrown to the lions has exercised a strong hold on the Christian psyche, though the *Catholic Encyclopaedia* casts doubt on its historical accuracy. That Christians were, on occasion, 'thrown to the lions' by the Roman emperors is not disputed, but the numbers involved most certainly are. The greatest of all Roman persecutors, Diocletian, who reigned from 284 to 305 AD, seems to have favoured either fire or the sword. One notorious, early persecutor, Nero, seems to have burned most of his Christian victims to death – not that Nero, a true connoisseur of torture, according to his many critics, neglected the

The elephant as executioner, efficiently dispatching a malefactor in India, as recorded by a French traveller in 1871. The hideousness of this form of punishment derives in part from the elephant's very gentleness as domesticated beast of burden, its obedient nature here used, perversely, to crush a human skull.

A high price to pay for carelessness – yet the Roman slave annoyed his aristocratic master at his peril. Here, a house slave of Vedius Pollio, a friend of the Emperor Augustus, is thrown into a tank of carnivorous eels for the offence of breaking his master's favourite crystal cup.

possibilities afforded by the animal kingdom. Tacitus's claim that the emperor dressed unfortunate prisoners in animal hides and then set his hunting dogs to attack and kill them is topped by Suetonius's story that, in fact, Nero had a predilection for cloaking himself in wolfskin and savaging his victims, tearing their private parts away with his own teeth.

Neither testimony would, of course, meet modern standards of historical, let alone legal, evidence; nor would the claims that Nero liked to watch living victims being eaten by an Egyptian crocodile he kept for the purpose; or that, for the crime of having dropped a drinking cup, he had one slave thrown into a pond of lampreys, a type of small eel with a formidable set of tiny, yet needle-sharp, teeth. These creatures allegedly swarmed all over the unfortunate man, ripping the flesh from his bones in a matter of moments.

Some Christians certainly do seem to have met their deaths in the arena, killed by wild animals of various kinds. A fascinating document describes the deaths of two sisters, Saint Perpetua and Saint Felicity, and other Christian martyrs, in the arena of Roman Carthage in 203 AD. The men were confronted with a boar, then a bear and finally a leopard. One, Saturus, had predicted that a leopard would kill him: miraculously, the first two beasts shrank away from him and left him well alone. In mock-deference to their sex, meanwhile, the sisters were attacked by a wild cow driven to a frenzy by cruelty and then released into the ring 'against all custom'.

Some Christians do seem to have met their deaths in the arena, killed by wild animals of various kinds

The cursed rat

Lions, leopards, bears, even a wild cow – all can be frightening, but few creatures can unsettle and disgust us as does the common or gutter rat. That there is some rational basis for this fear is obvious: The rat can spread diseases as well as deliver a nasty nip. The Tower of London with its pit of writhing rats only delivered, in concentrated form, a hazard many prisoners have had to face. When the humanitarian campaigner, John Howard, toured England's prisons in 1779, he found that the debtor's gaol in Knaresborough, Yorkshire, consisted of a single small room divided in half by an open sewer. In his book *The State of the Prisons*, published in 1784, he wrote: 'I was informed that an officer, confined here some years since, for a few days, took in with him a dog to defend him from vermin; but the dog was soon destroyed, and the prisoner's face much disfigured by them.'

The story of the torture by rats is well known (as immortalized in George Orwell's novel *Nineteen Eighty-Four*). The historian of torture George Ryley Scott, though adamant that the dreadful story is indeed a

A scene from Johan Sumpf's Chronicle of Switzerland *(1548). A condemned man is hung between two frenzied, famished dogs.*

matter of historical fact, is strikingly vague on the matter, suggesting only that the punishment was used 'at one time in Holland':

The victim was stripped, and tied hand and foot, face upwards, on top of a table or bench, or secured to stakes fixed in the ground. An iron vessel, of basin-like shape, containing several large dormice or rats,

was turned upside down upon the prisoner's stomach. The next step was to light a fire on top of the metal container. The animals, driven frantic by the heat and unable to escape, burrowed their way into the prisoner's entrails.

Cats and dogs

A related torture, says Scott, was inflicted by the Inquisition on the early Protestant heretics in Germany. In this case, cats were placed on the prisoner's abdomen, then goaded and prodded to attack his flesh. Cats also make their appearance in an obscure torture said to have been used in the 13th century, when a suspected witch might be placed in a sack with a number of these squalling, scratching creatures.

The use of dogs as torturers' assistants has been better documented. Every modern police force has its team of dogs, trained to attack in the line of work – a discipline that has all too easily been abused in the course of recent history. Although there seems to be no compelling evidence for the claim that the torturers of Pinochet's Chile trained Alsatian dogs to rape female prisoners, the threat of such violation appears to have been routinely made. Similar stories have been told by female Tibetan prisoners about their Chinese gaolers. Again, there has been no convincing confirmation, but dogs have certainly been used in Chinese prisons to attack helpless, sometimes naked, prisoners: one Buddhist monk is reported to have had his calf bitten off by one ferocious animal. The case recalls that of the sadistic Russian landowner Madame de Svirsky, whose egregious cruelty had, by 1853, gone too far even for the indulgent Tsarist court:

> She used to force her serfs to eat their excrement or rotted eggs. She used to strike them with an arapnik, or make them sit naked upon ice. She forced a little girl to eat a plait of hair. A wolf-bitch was kept in her courtyard, and she often set it upon the peasants. One woman was nearly killed by it; another received 30 wounds.

Ants, insects and other afflictions

An insect bite may pale into insignificance beside a wolf's, but *en masse* the stings of insects can be a terrible torture. 'George', a former political prisoner in China, described how he had been chained to an outdoor lamp-post overnight in the summer months, when dense clouds of mosquitoes would congregate each night to feed upon him. One 28-year-old Pakistani man taken into custody by his country's police found himself the subject of a bewildering variety of tortures: everything from

Cats were placed on the prisoner's abdomen, then goaded and prodded to attack his flesh

*Of all the persecutions
suffered by the Christian
martyrs for their faith,
few can have been as
bizarre as that of an
early prelate (depicted
here in a much later
engraving of 1807) who
was subjected to a
prolonged attack by a
swarm of deliberately
enraged bees.*

beating to electric shocks, from thermal to chemical burning. One of the cruelest techniques, however, was the application of a coat of viscous sugar-solution all over his body, which attracted stinging, biting insects in their droves.

Among those tortures the ANC is known to have employed in Angola was the practice of making prisoners sit for long periods on top of anthills, their bodies sometimes coated with a mix of honey and water to attract the insects. Another popular ANC torture was that of forcing captives to crawl through thickets of stinging plants. A similar ordeal was employed in Pinochet's Chile. Among several specimen charges laid against the general on his arrest in London in 1998 was that, in his capacity as Commander-in-Chief of the Chilean Army, he was responsible for the actions of those who had inflicted 'severe pain or suffering' on one Pedro Hugo Arellano Carvajal by 'placing him on board a helicopter, pushing him out with ropes tied to his trousers, and dragging him through thorns.'

Exposure in the afternoon sun can be a torture in itself in some climates, as it was for those pegged out on the ground by the Apaches during Geronimo's rising of 1874–86. In some hot countries today,

Bound to a wild stag, which, terrified at the unaccustomed weight and scent of its human rider, goes careering and crashing off through the densest thickets of the forest, the prisoner in this Russian scene faces an awful journey, which can only end in lingering death.

prisoners are not pinned down on the earth but left locked in derelict cars. But whatever its modern refinements, torture by exposure dates back at least as far as classical Rome's infamous Tarpeian Rock. This outcrop from which traitors were traditionally flung was not in fact high enough for the fall to kill outright: the Romans' purpose would have been defeated had their prisoners died so easily. Rather, the intention of the punishment was that the victims' arms and legs would be broken by the impact of their fall, leaving them to lie helpless on the earth below, hungering and thirsting as they burned slowly in the searing sun.

'What you saw was a bunch of buried trenches with people's arms and things sticking out of them'

Buried alive

Among the corpses buried in mass graves by Serb killers at Srebrenica, Bosnia, in 1992, many are believed to have been Muslims who were interred alive. During the Gulf War of 1991, American military engineers notoriously bulldozed occupied trenches, burying Iraqi conscripts in their hundreds, perhaps even in their thousands. 'I came through right after the Lead Company,' recalled Colonel Anthony Moreno, Commander of the First Mechanized Infantry Division's Second Brigade. 'What you saw was a bunch of buried trenches with people's arms and things sticking out of them.'

Iraq has been no stranger torture by live burial. When the ruling Baath Party first came to power (ironically, with the backing of the United States, its Gulf War enemy), it is believed to have buried many of its opponents alive in mass graves. In April 1998, meanwhile, the country's Shia opposition reported that a hundred prisoners had been bused from the capital's Radhwaniya Prison to an isolated spot in the countryside and forced into a pit where they were subsequently buried alive.

In the 13th-century, the same fate was meted out to the Cathars during the Albigensian Crusade. As late as 1460, a Parisian woman convicted of theft was condemned by the city's Provost to be 'buried alive before the gallows' of the French capital. Why such an extraordinary penalty should have been exacted for a comparatively minor crime is not reported. The crimes of the Central Asian tyrant Tamburlaine are legendary. After the surrender of Sivas in 1400 he is said to have buried alive the Christian city's entire garrison of 4000 troops. Among the ancient Slavs, living children were sometimes walled up in important buildings as they were being constructed: cruel as this unquestionably was, it was intended as a form of sacrifice to the gods and not, specifically, as an intentional act of torture. Less drastic, perhaps, but more consciously cruel was the game played by ANC

An excited crowd presses round as, resisting to the last, a Moroccan mass-murderer is immured and left to die in darkness. An extreme punishment, but then, according to the French magazine that published this picture in 1906, he had been convicted of killing no fewer than 30 women.

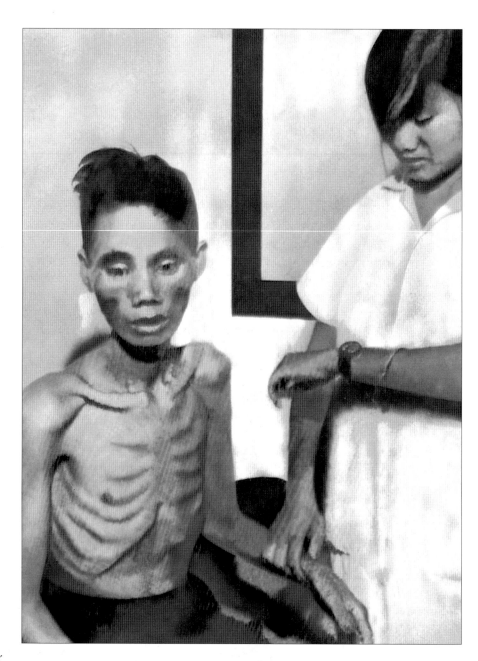

Starvation can be a torture in itself, as this 23-year-old Vietnamese man would discover when held in a North Vietnamese prison camp in the mountains of Phu Yen province. Here, after liberation, he is checked over by a nurse, but he is extremely fortunate to be alive at all.

forces in Angola, in which prisoners were placed in pits and pelted with stones as they attempted to climb out and save themselves. A report from El Salvador describes how up to 11 men were thrown down one deep well, dying slowly of starvation over succeeding days.

That starvation could in itself be a form of torture is illustrated vividly in literature by the case of real-life, 13th-century nobleman and turncoat, Ugolino della Gherardesca, who turns up in the lowest circle of Hell in Dante's *Divina Commedia*, chewing away for all eternity on the head of his tormentor, the Archbishop Ruggieri. An opportunist who had switched allegiance back and forth between the Pope and the Emperor's party, Ugolino was imprisoned in the Eagle Tower by his sometime ally, Ruggieri. Left to starve here with his two small sons, Ugolino had first had to undergo the grief of watching them die. After that, so the story went, he ended up eating his own flesh and blood in desperation. But if the deprivation of nourishment can be a torture, so too can the ingestion of food and drink.

An 18th-century report from British India describes how 'Murshid Aly Khan, who became Newab of Bengal in 1718, made defaulting zemindars drink buffalo milk mixed with salt, till they were brought to death's door by diarrhoea.' In 1635, Johann Matthaus Meyfarta described a strikingly similar sort of treatment being used by legally minded inquisitors who shrank from applying more extreme measures:

> The prisoners are fed only on salted food, and ... their drink is mixed with herring pickle, and no drop of pure, unadulterated wine, beer, or water is allowed them, but a raging thirst is purposely kept up in them ... but this cruel, raging, devouring thirst the inquisitors do not consider torture.

Less wholesome fare still has been provided by torturers in Communist China, where, immediately after 'liberation' in 1949, perceived opponents were rounded up and persecuted. According to testimony from ex-prisoners, one technique favoured at that time involved making prisoners eat excrement, one guard pulling back the victim's head, and holding his mouth open with a wooden pin while another spooned in faeces and/or urine. Now, new arrivals are forced to kneel before what in prison slang is known as the 'cassia blossom vase' – the toilet bucket – and suck up sewage through a straw. 'Does the

The grotesque instrument of a grim torture, this medieval mask features a long, funnelled tube through which the wearer might be cruelly force fed.

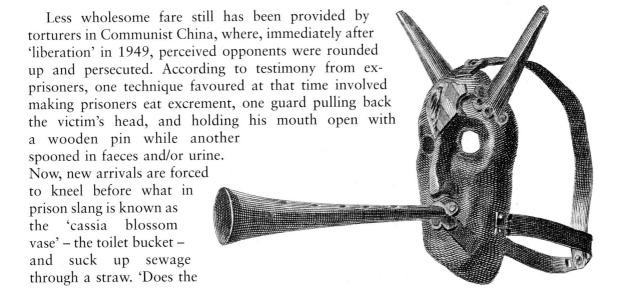

Early Rome reserved a brutal fate for those regarded as traitors to the Republic: here, as imagined by a 19th-century German artist, is a typical scene at the Tarpeian Rock.

cassia blossom taste sweet?' they are then asked. 'Delicious,' they must reply, or the experience will be repeated over and over till they have answered to their torturer's satisfaction.

That the alluring fragrance of the cassia blossom should be equated to the stench of the cessbucket is an unquestionably foul inversion. And it perhaps reveals – more than those particular communist prison guards would be happy to admit – that a hint of the perverse informs the quality of many acts of torture. In the chapters to come, we shall see how, at times, this hint becomes fully manifest sexual sadism.

A particularly exotic execution, as reported by the French traveller Coupin from Dahomey (now Benin), West Africa, in 1905: a parricide's head and shoulders are encaged in a tree's upper branches and his whole body is left to dangle.

Chapter Seven

Beating

The most basic of all brutalities, requiring no more than a flurry of blows with fists, and the kicking of feet, beating is torture at its simplest. The common currency of the schoolyard bully and the abusive policeman, of the military interrogator and the violent husband, beating has had a history far too long to be chronicled. The historian's difficulties are not eased by the huge differences of opinion there have been at different times and in different places over the question of where 'chastisement' has ended and 'torture' has begun. Corporal punishment, for example, is now considered taboo in schools, and domestic violence in any form is recognized as a crime. Compare this with the view expressed by the 18th-century legal writer William Blackstone that one of the humane glories of the English system was the law banning a husband from administering 'necessary correction' to his wife using any rod with a diameter greater than that of his thumb.

While beating would seem far too crude a business to require any sort of explanatory comment, it has still had its refinements, its cultural variations down the centuries. The account of 'Joao', rounded up with other suspected leftists in Santiago after General Pinochet's coup and interned in the Chile Stadium, describes two different approaches to beating used within just 24 hours:

> In these cases, they did not use the torture chambers but the baths. Groups of between ten and fifteen would enter the baths. They would beat their heads in with their rifle butts until … well … until their heads were squashed. Later they would send soldiers to clean up. Although they cleaned up, one could still see evidence of the violence, because there was blood on the walls and at times even chunks of flesh that had been splattered … by the type of blow administered.

Chile's torturers could be far more devious in their methods, as 'Joao' found out when it was his turn to be beaten: 'They hit me with a sort of rubber truncheon with a steel cable inside, which does not leave any marks. It does not leave any marks, but it causes internal damage.' The lasting evidence of cuts and bruises is one of the problems for torturers who beat their victims, yet need to keep their crimes secret from the public, press or international observers. They rely on a range of implements, including

A beating can be the most casual, ad hoc affair, or it can be dignified by official ritual. So it was in Wandsworth Prison, London, where this specially constructed whipping post was used in the 19th century.

*Beatings often played a
peripheral part in all
sorts of other tortures:
what else was breaking
on the wheel, after all,
but a beating taken to
its logical conclusion?
This nineteenth-century
engraving of an
execution by the
Inquisition underlines
the difficulty of judging
where one punishment
ended and another one
began.*

lengths of rubber tubing with sand, concrete or metal fillings, as well as sandbags, which inflict severe pain without leaving visible marks behind. (Dried bull penises, flexible but firm, were widely used in agrarian societies from medieval Europe to early 20th-century Mexico.)

Another means to the same end is an agonizing torture known as the *telefono* or 'telephone' – simply slapping the suspect's ears, which abruptly increases the pressure within the ear canal, thus threatening to burst the ear drum. Variations of this include the Haitian 'twin-slap', by which both ears are boxed simultaneously, as well as one used by the ANC in Angola in which prisoners were made to puff their cheeks out before beating, which increased the likelihood of rupturing their ear drums. A related torture, the 'bell', involves a metal drum or other container being placed over the victim's head and then banged loudly and continuously: the noise and vibrations are misery to endure.

In the face of international conventions on human rights, security forces in the state of Israel are allowed to apply only 'moderate pressure' – especially, it seems, pressure that leaves no incriminating marks. A 1995 report from Physicians for Human Rights (PHR) details one such instance:

> Two Israeli pathologists and a PHR consultant determined that a Palestinian prisoner 'died a violent and unnatural death' shortly after his arrest by Israeli security forces earlier this year … (Abdeld El Zasmet) Harizat, a computer specialist from Hebron, was arrested on suspicion of involvement with Muslim militants on 22 April. In the course of his interrogation, the investigators grabbed his shirt and shook him repeatedly on several occasions. Later, the investigators grabbed him by the shoulders and resumed the shaking. Healthy at the time of his arrest, Harizat was brought to Haddassah Hospital in a coma after his interrogation and was certified as brain dead less than 24 hours later.

The external autopsy report by Scottish doctor, Derrick Pounder, concluded that Harizat had no external marks to indicate any significant beating or kicking. But, he stated, both the brain haemorrhage from which Harizat died, and the bruising on his chest where he had apparently been gripped, suggested a death analogous to what has become known (after several notorious cases) as 'shaken baby syndrome'. The report continued:

> Based on the verbal testimony of released detainees, the most common form of direct violence used by General Security Service (GSS) interrogators is not blows or kicks but violent shaking whilst clutching

'Harizat was in a coma after his interrogation and was certified as brain dead less than 24 hours later'

the detainee by their collars or shoulders ... Ex-detainees describe the shaking as so vigorous and protracted that it produced loss of consciousness or severe neck pains for days afterward.

Excruciating in themselves, tortures that involve suspending the body also make it completely vulnerable to attack with sticks or lengths of cable or even, on occasion, iron bars. A variation used in some Middle Eastern countries, such as Turkey and Saudi Arabia, is that of suspending the body – sometimes upside down – from a revolving ceiling fan, a technique known as the 'helicopter'. In this and other restraint positions, the prisoner is unable to move his hands to ward off the raining blows. A prisoner might be tied down flat for beating, as on the Indian *manja*, an ordinary bed-frame, or upright, against a radiator or purpose-built wooden frame.

'They hung me from a wooden cross with my hands and arms tied with a rope'

> They hung me from a wooden cross with my hands and arms tied with a rope', testified one Chilean victim of torture. 'It is difficult to explain ... they placed me like a cross, but with my legs so far apart as if they intended me to do the splits. They started to beat me all over my body, especially the genitals.

One technique used by torturers in many countries is *la barra* or 'the bar', which is also known as *el pollo* or 'the chicken' in Spanish, or *o pau de arara*, 'the parrot's perch' in Portuguese. The suspect's wrists are tied round his bent knees, a pole is pushed between his knees, and the whole arrangement is suspended. The pain is intense; blood-supply and nervous communication to the legs are cut off, leaving the victim's body peculiarly vulnerable to all-over beating, especially *bastinado*.

Bastinado

In the torture of *bastinado*, or *falaka*, the prisoner is beaten on the soles of the feet, usually with the legs tied together in an upward position. Anything from a thick truncheon or the finest cane can be used, with agonizing results. Although a very localized assault, the pain in fact reaches quickly through the body right up to the head. The torture is redoubled when, after the beating, the victim is made to walk on rough ground, perhaps giving the heaviest guard a piggyback. When administered by a master-torturer, the lightest rhythmic rapping on the sole produces, over the course of a few minutes, the most maddening pain and mental anguish in the victim.

In countries such as Persia (now Iran) and Turkey, this was an officially sanctioned penalty for many centuries. The practice continues

East and West are united in brutality in this scene from the Russian–Chinese frontier, recorded by a French traveller in 1908: a thief is belaboured with an iron bar for stealing some fish.

Stretched out upon the ground, the soles of his bare feet saluting the sky, a Persian prisoner endures the torment of bastinado *in this 1896 engraving – at which time* bastinado *was still officially sanctioned.*

today in backroom tortures. Chinese torturers are said to have practised on blocks of bean curd (aiming to strike the surface without breaking the fragile skin) in order to develop the skills required to produce the most exquisite pain by means of the 'gentlest' beating. The same bamboo switches used on the feet for *bastinado* were also applied to the upper thighs and buttocks for more conventional canings, a punishment still on the statute book in many parts of the Far East. Historian Sir Henry Norman, while visiting China at the end of the 19th century, witnessed the trauma inflicted by an apparently trivial caning:

After a few more minutes of the dactyllic rap-tap-tap, rap-tap-tap, a deep groan broke from the prisoner's lips. I walked over to look at him, and whereas at first he had lain quiet of his own accord, now a dozen men were holding him tight.

Lengths of split bamboo, with their razor-sharp edges, could severely lacerate the skin. The trained torturer could tear the victim's flesh off in little strips. In the Philippines, the rattan, a type of palm plant, was used as an alternative to bamboo, its strong but flexible stem applied for the purposes of punishment.

Altogether cruder instruments of torture were the heavy wooden battledores, or battoirs – designed for beating wet clothes during washing – with which women in particular were beaten in the religious riots of early 19th-century France. At a time when Catholics were persecuting their Protestant neighbours, M. Durand, a Catholic lawyer, described the beatings he saw:

> The assassins in the faubourg Bourgade arm a battoir with sharp nails in the form of a fleur-de-lys; I have seen them raise the garments of females and apply with heavy blows to the bleeding body this battoir to which they gave a name which my pen refuses to inscribe. The cries of the sufferers – the streams of blood – the murmurs of indignation, which were suppressed by fear – nothing could move them. The surgeons who attended on those who are dead, can attest by the marks of their wounds, and the agonies which they endured, that this account, however, horrible, is most strictly true.

The whip's lash
Filipino worker Donato Lama gave this testimony to representatives of Amnesty International in 1999, two years after he was gaoled in Riyadh, Saudi Arabia for attending a secret Christian service:

> I was brought to the whipping area. They tied me to a post. My hands were handcuffed and they also shackled my legs. … The whip was one and a half metres long … with a heavy lead piece attached to the tip. It was terrible. Some fell on my thighs and my back. I would fall when the whip reached my feet but the prison guard would raise me up to continue the whipping. It was terrible. I was amazed to find myself still alive after the 70th lash was given. It lasted about 15 minutes … my back was bleeding. I cried.

The same punishment that Lama suffered has been inflicted on victims throughout the last three or four millennia. After the clenched fist or kick,

Lengths of split bamboo, with their razor-sharp edges, could severely lacerate the skin

and then the stick in all its multifarious forms, the whip was the first significant technological development in the gruesome science of beating.

The Romans whipped their slaves with such zeal that, according to the poet Horace, the executioner himself might collapse exhausted before the punishment was complete. For the most minor offences, the flat leather ferula was used, a mild enough punishment in its way, one familiar to many generations of British schoolchildren, and, indeed, for many decades to adult inmates of the Canadian prison system, before it was abolished in 1972).

More severe was the *scutica* – its lashing thongs were made of stiff parchment. But for the gravest floggings the dreadful *flagellum* was used, its long oxhide lashes knotted (or weighted with splinters of bone, metal balls, hooks or spikes) for intensified pain. Slaves often died beneath the *flagellum*, which was also used as a weapon in the gladiatorial arena. With the addition of the simple oxhide cart-whip, the main types of whip had already been developed in Roman times. The 'cat o'nine tails', with its metal-tipped thongs; the 'birch' with its rough and ragged birch-twig end; the Russian knout; the Jamaican cart-whip, and the similar *sjambok* used by South Africa's Boers: the implements that terrorized early-modern Europe and its colonies were all based on instruments already tried and tested in ancient Rome.

> *The Romans whipped their slaves with such zeal that the executioner himself might collapse exhausted*

Public flogging

The phenomenon of whipping as a public spectacle can also be dated back to ancient Rome, when those convicted of grave crimes were whipped as they made their way through the streets to their place of execution. The tradition of 'whipping at the cart's arse' (or cart's tail, as it was more delicately known) was already well established in Britain by the time of Henry VIII's 'Whipping Act', enacted in 1530. Officially called the Act Against Vagrants, it ordained that vagrants should be 'carried to some market town nearby ... and there tied to the end of a cart naked and beaten with whips [throughout that town] ... till the body shall be bloody by reason of such whipping.'

An amendment to this act, put through by Henry's daughter, Elizabeth I, modified the law by requiring that the victims should henceforth only be naked 'from the waist upward'.

The same punishment could be imposed for other crimes, as demonstrated in a case recorded in Salisbury in 1231:

> Thomas de Colne, one of the choristers of the Cathedral spent the night with the
> wife of an actor, in his house. The Dean went to investigate and she admitted she

Feeling the full ferocity of the knout, a prisoner is left in no doubt where authority lies in the absolutist empire of the Russian Tsars. This image dates from 1901, at a time when tension was building steadily through a spiralling cycle of mounting discontent and official crackdown.

had been having an affair with Thomas for more than a year and came often to him in the Close by night and day, whenever he wished ... she was ordered to be whipped through the Close and out into the city.

The perjurer Titus Oates is flogged at the cart's tail from the prison at Newgate to the scaffold at Tyburn in 1685. In fact, though his concocted 'evidence' saw many hanged, he escaped the gallows to die a respected figure.

As so often with medieval punishments, the humiliating public exhibition was an important element, but the flogging itself would certainly have been a horrible torture.

The first Quaker evangelists, for example, often fell foul of the 'Whipping Act'. In England the custom of whipping through the streets was gradually superceded by that of flogging at fixed whipping-posts in busy market squares. In 1653, the Quaker preachers Mary Fisher and Elizabeth Williams were accordingly whipped, as 'whores', at the market cross in Cambridge. Quakers in the American colonies

would find these English traditions still prevailed in New England as late as 1657:

> Mary Tomkins and Alice Ambrose were cruelly ordered to be whipped at a cart's tail through 11 towns at one time, 10 stripes apiece on their naked backs, which would have amounted to 110 in the whole, and on a very cold day, they were stripped and whipped through three of the towns … till Walter Barefoot, of Salisbury, got the warrant and discharged them.

In Scotland, as in England, whippings were an everyday part of the civic scene. In Banff in 1629, for instance, Isobel Mitchell was 'ordanit to be presentlie strippet naikit and scourged out of this burgh and perpetuallie banischit' for thieving. Although over time, whipping came to be a sentence handed down principally for the 'crime' of vagrancy, it was also inflicted on many women whose 'wanderings' were sexual in nature. In Aberdeen in 1640, for example, Margaret Warrack was ordered to be flogged at the stake so that she might be persuaded publicly to confess her crime of 'fornication'.

The slavedriver's whip

The life of the New World slave was, as one historian has said, from start to finish little more than 'one long torture'. Those who avoided the trauma of being captured and abducted from their homelands and crammed into stinking ships' holds for the Atlantic passage had the heartbreaking ignominy of being born into bondage. Quite literally the property of the plantation owners, they were, for the most part, even deprived even of the normal bonds of kinship: neither couples nor families with children had any status in the masters' eyes. They were bought and sold at will, were punished savagely at any caprice, and, in their daily work, were whipped as though recalcitrant animals.

It was a cruel punishment, but flogging was so far from being unusual for slaves that only in extreme cases does it seem to have elicited any comment – cases like that of the Jamaican cook stripped and personally flogged by her master, the Reverend G.W. Bridges in 1829 until she was a 'mass of lacerated flesh and gore'. Her offence was to have killed a turkey, on Bridges' own instructions, for a dinner guest who failed to show. The Reverend Bridges was summoned to appear in court, but despite all the evidence of witnesses and the woman's injuries, he was acquitted. From the facts of this case, it seems inescapable that flogging could be motivated more by intense sexual sadism than by any genuine

The life of the New World slave was from start to finish little more than 'one long torture'

'need' to maintain discipline or impose order. Other cases, meanwhile, seem to have stemmed from a more generalized tyranny.

A House of Commons committee was told in 1814 how a certain Mr Huggins had publicly subjected '21 of his slaves, men and women, to upwards of 3000 lashes of the cartwhip' in the marketplace at Nevis, Jamaica. One of the women suffered 291 strokes and one of the men no fewer than 365. Slaves were often 'bowsed out', in the seafaring slang – bound at wrists and ankles and then stretched out with a rope and pulley. This sort of treatment, which was often followed with a caning, was justified on the grounds that it helped to 'beat out the bruised blood'.

The instruments of flogging varied from place to place. A visitor to a West African port saw a newly captured slave being whipped with a lash made of manatea or manatee – the hide of the sea elephant – but the implements used were pretty much on a par when it came to their grim inhumanity. Typical of the kind of cart-whip used every day, without a moment's reflection in plantations up and down the New World, was the one described by Austin Steward, a former-slave in the American South:

> The overseer always went around with a whip, about nine feet [2.8m] long, made of the toughest kind of cowhide, the butt-end of which was loaded with lead, and was about four or five inches [10 or 12cm] in circumference, running to a point at the opposite extremity. This made a dreadful instrument of torture and, when in the hands of a cruel overseer, it was truly fearful. With it, the skin of an ox or a horse could be cut through. Hence, it was no uncommon thing to see the poor slaves with their backs mangled in a most horrible manner.

Another escaped American slave, Moses Grandy, recalled of his master:

> MacPherson would sometimes tie the slave's shirt over his head, that he might not flinch when the blow was coming: sometimes he would increase his misery, by blustering and calling out that he was coming to flog again, which he did or did not, as happened. I have seen him flog slaves with his own hands, till their entrails were visible; and I have seen the sufferers dead when they were taken down. He never was called to account in any way for it.

Crueller still, though, was the white masters' way of making black slaves take on the role of one another's abusers. The father of Francis Fedric, a Virginia slave who escaped to the North and, ultimately, to England, remembered how his father, appointed overseer by the master, had been ordered to flog his own mother:

'I have seen him flog slaves with his own hands, till their entrails were visible'

My grandmother having committed the crime of attending a prayer meeting, was ordered to be flogged by her own son. This was done by tying her hands before her with a rope, and then fastening the rope to a peach tree, and laying bare the back. Her own son was then made to give her 40 lashes with a thong of a raw cow's-hide, her master standing over her the whole time blaspheming and threatening what he would do if her son did not lay it on.

A grim example to others, a criminal is publicly whipped in London's Sessions House Yard, circa 1745.

A soldier prepares to run the gauntlet of his eager 'comrades' in this engraving made in 1534.

Unfortunately, even freedom did not release black Americans from the threat of flogging. As late as 1851, in Yankee Boston, blacks who ventured onto the streets after nightfall were liable to be arrested and given 39 lashes.

Military beatings

In previous centuries, enlistment in the armed forces of the major military powers may have seemed like slavery, and never more so than in matters of punishment for disciplinary offences. Even today, initiation rituals in armies the world over – sometimes savage – reinforce an ethos of unrelieved machismo. In the past, even official punishments often amounted to little more than glorified beatings. Offenders were often punched and kicked as they were made to run the gauntlet between lines of their comrades. In one case in the British Garrison at Tangier, on 17 May 1665, sentence was passed on a soldier stipulating that he was:

> At the time of the parade to have his back stripped and to run the gauntlet of his regiment paraded with open ranks, each man furnished with a stout switch to strike the prisoner's back, breast, arms or where his cudgel should light as he marched down the lanes.

After the Mutiny Act of 1689, the 'cat o' nine tails' became a daily part of life in the British Army for two centuries. Its leather thongs were at first knotted, then afterwards weighted with steel spikes or hooks, for greater ferocity. As ever, public humiliation was an essential part of the punishment, and the offender was therefore scourged before the assembled ranks of his regiment, a drum beat keeping time throughout his torture, and partially covering his cries. The maximum punishment allowed was 1000 lashes, and anything between 500 and 800 strokes was routine. It was by no means rare for soldiers to die after such sustained whippings. When prisoners passed out, the torture was suspended, but it resumed a few days later once the victims had recuperated. Severe sentences were in any case broken down into separate bouts of, say, 200 lashes, to be administered at intervals of several days. This was a 'humanitarian' rule but, in effect, it merely added to the physical suffering of the actual torture, the agony of anticipation.

The expectation that the newly independent United States of America might match its democratic ideals with comparatively humane treatment (at least for free-born whites) finds some confirmation in the *Orderly Book of Jacob Turner*, an officer with Washington's Army between 1777 and 1778. Though by modern standards the punishments involved still seem frightful, the military tribunal shows clear signs of having at least considered the details and mitigating circumstances of the cases that passed before it:

Herman Wineocock of the German Regt charged with neglecting his duty and

After the Mutiny Act of 1689, the 'cat o' nine tails' became a daily part of life in the British Army for two centuries

absenting himself from his company and refusing to take his arms and accoutrements. The court after considering the charge and evidences are of opinion that the prisoner is guilty of all the charges exhibited but that of mutiny. Sentenced the prisoner to have 39 lashes on his bare back ... Solomon Grant of the 14th Virginia Regt charged with sleeping on his post pleaded guilty, and sentenced to receive 25 lashes on his bare back, but it appearing in evidence that he was a good, orderly, well behaved soldier and that he was probably unwell when on sentry the Commander in Chief remits the punishment.

Flogging round the fleet

Under Captain Hugh Pigot's command, the flogging of 'a dozen men a day' was said to be 'not unusual'

At sea, it was argued, the need for discipline was overwhelming and justified the most draconian system of punishments imaginable. Crew members considered slow to jump to an order or sluggish in applying themselves to a task were regularly 'started' with a stroke from a cane or switch by the bosun's mate. For graver offences flogging was frequent and fearsome. Under Captain Hugh Pigot's command of HMS *Hermione*, at the end of the 18th century, for example, the flogging of 'a dozen men a day' was said to be 'not unusual'.

The 'cat' as used in the Royal Navy was made not of leather but of a frayed rope's end, the disparate strands being plaited and knotted for greater flaying power. Alternatively, a cruder implement could be fashioned for one-time use by attaching 'tails' of fine cord to a handle of thick rope – though such an improvised scourge was still capable of breaking an inch-thick wooden board. The whole ship's company was assembled for the flogging, which took the form of a ceremony, with the officers in dress uniform and the marines and crew lined up in order. The offender was tied to an upturned grating and the captain read out the particular Article of War that had been broken before the bosun's mate stepped up to administer the punishment. A dozen strokes was standard for ordinary offences, but worse floggings were often enforced – and if such was the case, two bosun's mates took turns, each laying on 12 lashes at a time.

In theory, captains were supposed to take the most serious offences to an Admiralty Court, so had no business imposing more than a few dozen lashes on their own account, but few sailors felt it was in their interests to complain. Perhaps precisely to pre-empt such appeals, Naval Courts were notoriously severe in the sentences they handed out. On the whole, a man was well advised to take his captain's punishment, however excessive it might seem. The tradition of 'flogging round the fleet' was reserved for the most serious offences. The victim was subjected to separate, full-dress whippings on every naval ship in port.

On completion of each bout, he was placed in a smaller boat and rowed across to the next ship in line, and so on until every company in the fleet had had a chance to witness his pain and humiliation. With just such elaborate procedures as these, have men managed to pass off as judicious punishment what can, in truth, only be characterized as brutal torture.

Nothing undermined slaves' morale more than being forced into complicity in one another's oppression.

Chapter Eight

Cutting and Piercing

The executioner ambled forward in the flickering torchlight, his basket of blades clinking beneath his arm at every pace – in front of him, the prisoner stiffened, his mouth gaping wide in a silent scream. He set down the basket by his side and, sizing up his victim with a glance, reached down into his basket and randomly selected a blade. A pictogram picked out in its wooden handle told him which part of his victim's body to cut – in this case the gristle of the nose. There was a glint of metal and the hiss of severed flesh. The prisoner had found his voice now: no other sound could be heard over his chilling screams. His tormentor worked on unheeding, attacking an ear, a nipple, an arm. Strip by strip, he sliced and trimmed, carving away at a living, breathing man as though he were whittling wood …

Lingering death

Although imaginary, this scene captures the horrors associated with the Chinese *lingchi*, or 'lingering death'. As with other notorious Oriental tortures, however, the nature of *lingchi* has almost certainly been exaggerated in Western lore. What has become known as 'death by a thousand cuts' (and in some versions even ten thousand) is, say some experts, unlikely to have involved much more than three. According to the 19th-century historian Sir Henry Norman (author of *The People and Politics of the Far East*, published in 1895), the 'lingering death' was a matter of historical fact, yet he maintained there was a rational, rather than random, order of cutting, in which the fleshiest parts of the body (breasts, thighs, etc.) were followed by digits, extremities and joints.

Sir Ernest Alabaster, a scholar of Oriental law, argued that *lingchi* was not primarily aimed at causing physical suffering. It was, he conceded, an unthinkable torment, but mainly on religious and psychological grounds:

> This punishment … is not inflicted so much as a torture, but to destroy the future as well as the present life of the offender – he is unworthy to exist longer either as a man or a recognisable spirit, and, as spirits to appear must resume their present corporeal forms, he can only appear as

Spanish colonists bring 'civilization' and Christianity to the New World, as witnessed by Fray Bartolommé de las Casas in his eloquent and impassioned (if factually less than completely reliable) Brief Account of the Destruction of the Indies *(1552).*

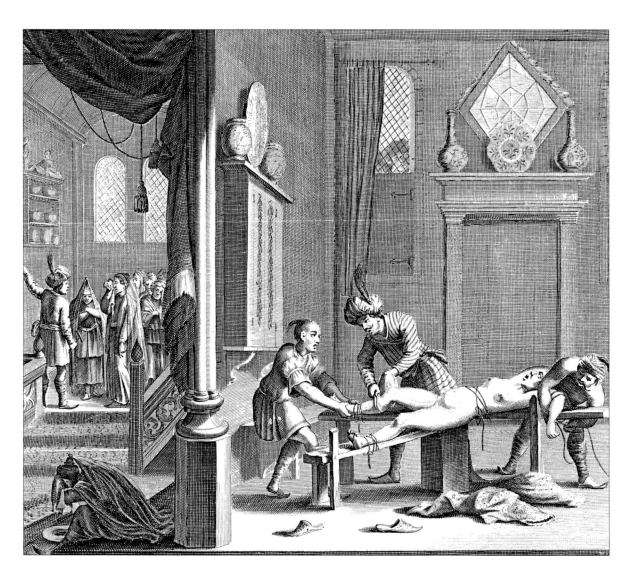

Oriental cruelty, as imagined by a late 17th-century German artist: torturers lay out a woman on a wooden framework to be flayed alive; in the background, a colleague shows off an earlier trophy.

a collection of little bits. It is not a lingering death, for it is all over in a few seconds, and the *coup de grâce* is generally given with the third cut; but it is very horrid, and the belief that the spirit will be in need of sewing up in a land where needles are not, must make the unfortunate victim's last moments most unhappy.

Stabbing and mutilation

The Roman emperor Caligula is said by Suetonius to have ordered executions along lines similar to those of the traditional Chinese 'death of a thousand cuts'. By subjecting prisoners to a series of small stab wounds, Caligula maintained, they would be able to 'feel themselves die'. In another of his punishments, however, he appears to have acted more in keeping with what would become known as the Judaeo-Christian tradition: when he ordered a thief's hands to be cut off and hung round his neck in token of his crime.

'Wherefore if thy hand or thy foot offend thee, cut them off, and cast them from thee: it is better for thee to enter into life halt or maimed, rather than having two hands or two feet to be cast into everlasting fire.' This famous quote from Matthew's Gospel, chapter 18, verse 8, suggesting that sins can symbolically be purged by mutilation, echoes the Old Testament ruling of 'an eye for an eye, a tooth for a tooth'. Although the literal practice of this concept is not a central part of Judaeo-Christian tradition, it has underscored events from Caligula's punishment of the thief to the injury endured by John Wayne Bobbitt at the hands of his wife Lorena in 1993 (she cut off his penis), to the state-approved 'judicial' amputations carried out in Islamic Saudi Arabia. In fact, the general idea of mutilation as punishment is at least as old as the ancient Indian text the *Laws of Manu*, which ordained as long ago as 1500 BC that certain crimes against the community should be punished this way: 'He who sells for seed-corn that which is not seed-corn; he who takes up seed already sown, and he who destroys a boundary-mark, shall be punished by mutilation.'

In the traditional account of St Agatha's martyrdom around 250 AD, her torture culminates with her breasts being cut off, symbolizing the crudest affront to her femininity. The existence in early-modern Europe of what appear to be specialized, iron 'breast rippers', which could be used either cold or hot, suggests that St Agatha's fate was by no means unique. Another symbolic punishment was that inflicted on Pope Leo III in 802 AD. He was waylaid in the street and abducted by kinsmen of his rival, Pope Adrian I, who blinded him and tore out his tongue to make him unfit for his office. The story goes that God saved his sight and speech by a miracle and he was able to witness and spread the Word just as before.

The association between crime and body part is evident in the 8th-century *Byzantine Ecloga* of sexual crimes, which ordained the penalty of castration for the 'abominable crime' of homosexuality. However, it recommended that when a couple are found in adultery, both parties should have their noses slit. In this case, mutilation was seen as a mark of public dishonour, its function to all intents and purposes the same as that of a brand. The notion of a literal correspondence between crime

'If thy hand or thy foot offend thee, cut them off, and cast them from thee...'

and punishment proved enduring. In his *Historia Calamitatum* (circa 1132), the 12th-century French theologian Peter Abelard recorded his own awful punishment at the hands of his young lover's family:

> Violently incensed, they laid a plot against me, and one night while I all unsuspecting was asleep in a secret room in my lodgings, they broke in with the help of one of my servants whom they had bribed. There they had vengeance on me with a most cruel and most shameful punishment, such as astounded the whole world; for they cut off those parts of my body with which I had done that which was the cause of their sorrow.

Prostitutes would continue to have their noses slit well into the 18th century

Medieval Europe was, for the most part, less precise in its punishments. England's William I ('the Conqueror') appears to have indiscriminately ordered the gouging out of eyes, slitting of noses and severing of ears. Five hundred years later in the reign of Elizabeth I, the law prescribed different punishments for thieves who repeatedly offended: one ear severed for a first offence, the other severed for a second and, finally, death for a third. Prostitutes would continue to have their noses slit well into the 18th century. As with so many cruel practices, that of mutilation survived far longer in the colonies than 'at home' – though alongside the more symbolic cuts, slave owners introduced the practice of severing the Achilles tendons of persistent runaways.

There may well have been administrative reasons for not castrating sexual offenders or cutting off the hands of thieves: All such amputations are by their very nature extremely dangerous, even with the benefits of modern surgical practice. When, in 1994, a group of police officers in Barmer, in the Indian state of Rajasthan, cut off the penis of a man accused of kidnapping his employer's daughter, they claimed his injuries were the result of a botched suicide attempt. The authorities were not convinced, however, and took proceedings against them.

Amnesty International estimates that at least 90 judicial amputations were carried out in Saudi Arabia between 1981 and 1999, yet an experienced executioner still confessed to anxieties over the practice. In an 1989 interview with an Arab journalist for the publication *al-Madina al-Munawwara*, he explained:

> For me it is more difficult to cut off a hand than to carry out an execution, because executions are done momentarily by the sword and the person leaves this life. By contrast, severing a hand demands more courage, especially because you are cutting off the hand of someone who

Those who raised their hands against the rule of Menelik, the late 19th-century Ethiopian ruler, could expect to have them hung around their necks as mementoes of their folly.

Still, somewhat improbably, sporting his bishop's mitre, a martyr is scientifically 'drawn' in this 16th-century woodcut, an ingenious crank arrangement carefully unravelling his intestines.

will remain alive afterwards, and also you have to cut it off at a specific joint and use your skill to make sure that the cutting implement stays in position.

Piercing pain

No device looms larger in the popular folklore of torture than the Iron Maiden, in whose embrace only agonizing death is found. Basically a female form fashioned from sheet iron, it opens at the front to allow the victim to be placed inside, and is lined throughout with inward-thrusting spikes. These are cunningly arranged so as to pierce all the most sensitive body parts. But did such a machine ever actually exist?

According to the testimony of a certain Colonel Lehmanowsky, the Spanish Inquisition used an Iron Maiden which it likened to the Virgin Mary. French writer Frederic Shoberl shed more light in his account of the Inquisition, the *Persecutions of Popery* (1844):

> …two ecclesiastics earnestly admonished him [the prisoner], in the presence of the Mother of God, to make a confession. 'See,' said they, 'how lovingly the blessed Virgin opens her arms to thee! On her bosom thy hardened heart will be melted; there wilt thou confess.' All at once, the figure began to raise extended arms: the prisoner, overwhelmed with astonishment, was led to her embrace; she drew him nearer and nearer, pressed him almost imperceptibly closer, till the spikes and knives pierced his breast.

This episode makes a good story, but concrete evidence for the existence of the device was slow to emerge. It was only around the middle of the 19th century that a so-called Virgin, or Jungfer, was actually found – and even then it is hard to be sure that the Iron Maiden of Nuremberg, discovered in an antiquarian collection, was anything more than a curiosity, made specially to supply the late 18th-century Gothic craze for such oddities. A document dating from August 1515 does, however, claim to show the Iron Maiden in action on a suspected forger. The doors, it says, shut

> slowly, so that the very sharp points penetrated his arms, and his legs in several places, and his belly and chest, and his bladder and the root of

his member, and his eyes, and his shoulders, and his buttocks, but not enough to kill him; and so he remained making great cry and lament for two days, after which he died.

Use of the Iron Maiden may remain historically doubtful, but other forms of torture by piercing have been well documented. In the early 1970s, prisoners marched through the streets to their place of execution, in the city of Da Tong in China's Shanxi province, were made to wear a wooden 'death tag'– attached by a clip running through the flesh of their necks – bearing their name. An Amnesty International report describes

This example of a 'medieval' Iron Maiden from Nuremberg may, in reality, be little older than the 19th-century woodcut depicting it.

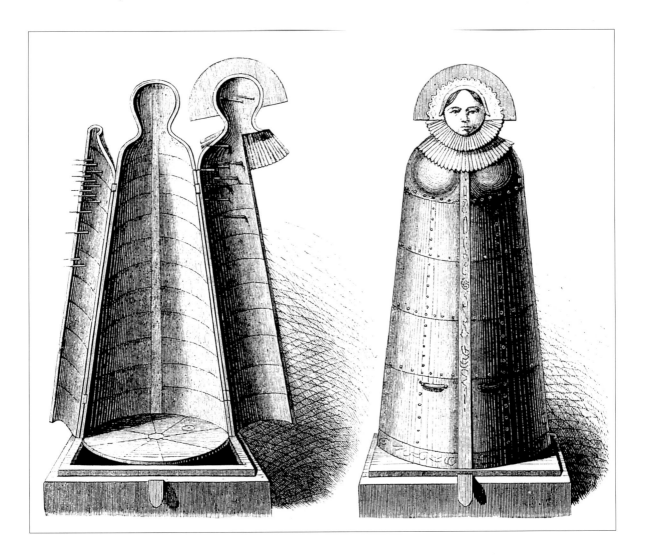

how in 1997 one Tamil prisoner of the Sri Lankan government had a nailed plank knocked into his hand and foot. Others had their extremities pierced by means of an electric drill. An Algerian Army conscript described in an interview with the British journalist Robert Fisk how he had seen power drills in action against suspected Islamic activists: 'Reda fidgets with his hands as he tells his awful story. The drills were used on the prisoners' legs. Reda says he saw one army torturer drill open a man's stomach. It lasted four hours with each prisoner …'

Spiked chariot-wheels make mincemeat of unfortunate victims in an 18th-century engraving that may well owe more to the mythic imagination than to reliable history.

Subsequent medical examinations (including X-ray evidence of a punctured lung) were found to confirm a Kashmiri Arabic teacher's claim in 1991 that an iron rod inserted into his rectum by Indian interrogators had been pushed all the way through to his chest. Such a

violation clearly takes us into the realm of sexual sadism. Symbolically, of course, all piercings of the body can be seen as analogous to sexual penetration (and certainly, at the most literal level, torture has tended to go together, down through history, with rape). The alleged insertion of a heated iron bar into the vagina of a woman prisoner by Chilean interrogators in the wake of Pinochet's coup echoes the execution of the homosexual English King Edward II by means of a red-hot poker up his rectum. So too, in its small way, does the practice employed by other Chilean torturers of extinguishing cigarettes in the anuses of detainees.

The 'pear' was used extensively in early-modern Europe, and is said to be still in use in many other parts of the world. This small metal device was inserted into the throat, vagina or rectum, and, when a screw was turned by an executioner in the course of questioning, its sharpened segments expanded causing crippling internal lacerations. But such specialized equipment is by no means necessary for torture: truncheons, bottles, thick cabling and all manner of other implements have been used for assaults of this kind – assaults that involve as much humiliation for the victim as they do excruciating pain.

Tearing

Another famous piercing punishment is that attributed to Oriental torturers who would spread-eagle a prisoner over a bed of growing bamboo. Over the ensuing days, the victim had to endure the torment of the surging shoots sprouting upward through his living flesh. How well any plant would actually grow in this case is, of course, very doubtful in the first place, and in the absence of any reliable evidence this would seem to be another torture worthy only of consiging to the category of 'colourful myth'. The piercing properties of bamboo have been well documented, though, when it comes to placing sharpened slivers under the victim's toe- or fingernails. This is perhaps the most frequently reported torture in the testimony of former prisoners held in Japanese camps during World War II.

The insertion of sharp splinters or points beneath prisoners' nails is a peculiarly painful and demoralizing torture, and one of the most ancient on record. It was given a new twist by agents of the Bolsheviks, who used gramophone needles to torture their White Russian opponents during the Civil War of 1918–19. A cruder torture is to simply tear off the toe- and fingernails at the quick. No modern torturer's toolkit is complete, therefore, without an ordinary pair of pliers, which can be applied not only to the nails but to nipples and other tender parts. Reports of such practices have come from the Middle and Far East,

The insertion of sharp splinters or points beneath prisoners' nails is a peculiarly painful and demoralizing torture

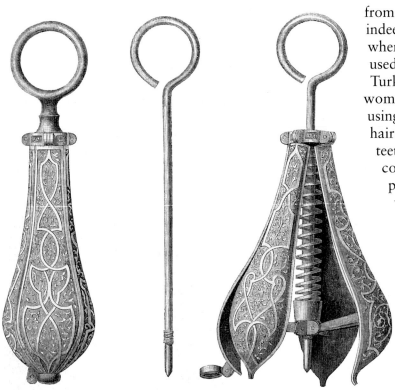

The aptly named poire d'angoisser, *or pear of anguish, certainly spelled agony for those who endured it, its sharp-edged sections expanding inexorably, deep into the mouth, rectum or vagina.*

from South America and Africa – indeed from just about every country where torture has extensively been used. From the Kurdish areas of Turkey come reports of police tying women prisoners' legs apart and using tweezers to pull out their pubic hairs one by one. The pulling of teeth as a means of torture has, of course, been known, and practised, since medieval times, while extractions by means of pliers or more specialized equipment, such as the use, without anaesthetic, of the dentist's drill, are frequently mentioned in accounts of modern torture. (The latter was memorably dramatized in cinematic fiction in the 1970s in *Marathon Man*, starring Dustin Hoffman and the late Laurence Olivier.)

Pricking witches

A curious footnote to torture history is the traditional and long-held practice of 'pricking' witches. This was not, in theory at least, about the infliction of pain but, on the contrary, the discovery of insensible spots. The great 17th-century witch-hunter Matthew Hopkins described how, in 1644, a fellow 'Discoverer'

had some seven or eight of that horrible sect of Witches living in Towne where he lived, a Towne in Essex called Maningtree with divers other adjacent Witches of other Townes, who every six weeks in the night (being alwayes on the Friday night) had their meeting close by his house, and had their severall solemne sacrifices there offered to the devill, one of which this discoverer heard speaking to her Imps one night, and bid them goe to another Witch, who was thereupon apprehended, and searched by women who had for many yeares knowne the Devills marks, and found to have three ceats upon her, which honest women have not …

The 'ceats' were said to be extra nipples for suckling 'imps', the Devil's children, and were generally agreed to 'feele neither pin, needle, aule, &c. thrust through them'. A high-sounding pseudo-science purported to distinguish them from 'naturall wretts on severall parts of their bodies, and other naturall excressencies, as Hemerodes, Piles, Childbearing, &c.' Professional 'prickers', qualified in making such distinctions, made a good living by travelling the country examining the bodies of suspected witches for the supposed marks of Satan. It was obviously in their interests to find them, and indeed they were generally successful in their search – if only because their victim, to put an end to this nagging torture, would eventually stop crying out in pain.

Insult is added to serious injury as, strung out agonizingly upon the rack, prisoners' bodies are given a cruel combing in this illustration from an 18th-century account of ancient tortures.

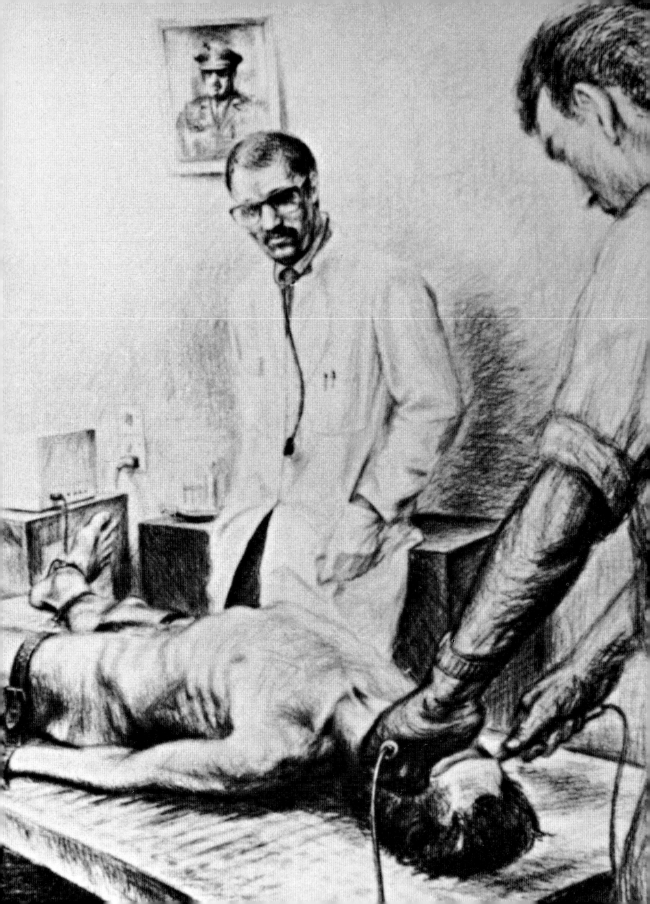

Chapter Nine

Shock Tactics

The electric chair has been used to execute prisoners in the United States since 1890, yet the application of electricity specifically as a form of torture is a far more recent development. Why this gap? Electricity's appeal as a means of torture would have been obvious from the very first, but the problem for torturers was technological: how to administer electric shocks sufficient to traumatize victims without killing them. The science of electric-shock torture is simple: it is not the voltage that is critical; it is the number of amps that is the real indicator of danger.

Electric stun devices, for example, can deliver shocks in excess of 200,000 volts, but at such a low amperage that the victim's life is not immediately threatened. The balancing of high voltage with low amperage was not easily attained. It took decades of development before the difficulty was resolved – to the torturer's advantage. Another reason for the comparatively slow emergence of electricity in torture was the lack of any perceived need. There were so many other age-old methods in the catalogue of cruelty that the addition of another weapon to an already overflowing arsenal scarcely seemed necessary.

Damage concealed

A 1991 Amnesty International report illustrates the use of electrical torture at its worst. It outlines the case of Roberto, a 50-year-old university professor living as a refugee in Zaire, who was taken into detention by security forces and badly beaten. After a short time, however, a senior officer arrived and told his tormentors to stop: 'It will leave scars,' he said, 'and we will get complaints from Amnesty International.' During the next four weeks, therefore, Roberto's captors never once laid fist or foot on their prisoner. Instead, they applied electroshock batons to the base of his spine, his genitals and other areas, heaping humiliation on top of excruciating pain. 'On most occasions,' the report said, 'he vomited, lost control of his bowels and bodily functions and fell unconscious.'

Electrocution is the quintessentially modern torture, by dint of the technology involved and the fact that it can be concealed from international law and the media. In a modern age in which aid packages and commercial contracts are increasingly tied (at least in theory) to a

The last word in modern, forward-looking, technocratic torture, right down to the white-coated doctor standing by, this view of electroshock 'treatment' is based on the accounts of Chilean survivors.

regime's commitment to upholding conventions on human rights, electrical torture has that most important of political virtues: 'deniability'. In fact, electroshock torture does quite frequently leave lasting traces. It remains the case, however, that these small reddish patches are easily missed by cursory inspection, unlike the distinct scars left by cigarette burns or the livid bruises that appear in the aftermath of beating. Hence the correlation, pointed out by some commentators, between the upsurge in the use of such techniques since the early 1970s and the rise of international concern over human rights.

Pariah nations unconcerned by international pressure initially had no need of electroshock torture. The former Soviet Union, for example, does not appear to have used it much. Contemptuous of western political opinion and of any views its own citizens might have had at home, the Soviet's Communist rulers saw no need to supercede their preferred method: beating. Nor did the Nazis, who were quite at ease with their notoriety, and with their existing methods of delivering brutality. Surprisingly, perhaps, the pioneers of electrical torture in the 20th century were not Stalin, Hitler, Mao, Mussolini or Franco, or any of the other likely candidates presiding over a repressive regime, but the democratic French.

From a therapeutic to a farming model, the shift towards versions of the picana, *or cattle prod, allowed the clean efficiency of electrode equipment to be combined with complete portability.*

The unravelling of the old French Empire – first in Indochina in the 1950s and then in Algeria – put a great strain on a nation that prided itself on being progressive and powerful. In the case of Algeria, French patriotism and liberalism went so much hand in hand that this North African country was regarded as being an integral part of the mother-country, rather than simply a colony. This attitude did not survive long in the face of the bitter war of independence that broke out towards the end of 1954. The temptation to use torture was, in the heat of conflict, altogether too strong to resist, yet the French were sensitive about how such treatment would appear to the watching world. Hence the 'hugger-mugger' torture of suspected *fels* (as the French settlers referred to the Algerian rebels) and the favouring of electrical methods considered to leave no scars.

Frantz Fanon recorded his experiences as a psychiatrist in Algeria in his book, *The Wretched of the Earth*, published in 1961. It documented the

注意：不使用时应存放在小
体及无关人员触摸
到的地方

WD1ELECTRIC SHOCK GUN

JING JIANG RADIO NO.4 FACTORY JIANGSU

dreadful, long-term, psychological and physiological effects of electrical torture:
These included everything from the almost unbearable sense of injustice to purely physical symptoms of 'localized or generalized coenesthopathies ... "pins and needles" throughout their bodies; their hands seemed to be torn off, their heads seemed to be bursting, and their tongues felt as if they were being swallowed.' But there were no bleeding wounds or multicoloured bruises to be shown to the world's press. In that respect, the use of electrical torture was effective.

Miniaturization has been as vital in the development of new, technologically advanced instruments of torture as anywhere else – as this neat little baton, made in China in 1993, very clearly illustrates.

The French ran their torture devices off car batteries or field telephones, or off the hand-cranked dynamo, or magneto, either wrapping the electrodes round their subject's penis, ear, ankle or other extremity, or placing one electrode in a fixed position and using the other to range about the body's most sensitive parts. The charges involved were not enormous, but were precisely balanced between high voltage and negligible current in amps. It was, as one US marine trained in French techniques could testify, 'extremely painful'. How successful it was in the long run is, of course, highly debatable. France lost its colony, and the 'secret' of France's conduct could not be kept indefinitely. Given the alienation of the Algerian population and France's increasing isolation in the international community of the day, it is fair to say – as one French agent subsequently did – that, while these tortures had won his country the Battle of Algiers, they had caused France to lose the moral war.

From therapy to torture

One particularly sinister form of electric torture has its origins in the electric shock therapy used in psychiatric hospitals, as illustrated by the case of Teresa Meschiati, arrested by Argentinian security forces at Cordoba in 1976. She later recounted her ordeal to the National Commission on the Disappeared:

Though long since superseded in the wider world, this 1950s-style field telephone (as used in French Indo-China and Algeria) is still in use as an instrument of torture in contemporary Turkey.

Immediately after my arrival at La Perla … I was taken to the torture room or 'intense therapy' room. They stripped me and tied my feet and hands with ropes to the bars of a bed, so that I was hanging from them. They attached a wire to one of the toes of my right foot. Torture was applied gradually, by means of electric prods of two different intensities: one of 125 volts which caused involuntary muscle movements and pain all over my body. They applied this to my face, eyes, mouth, arms, vagina, and anus; and another of 220 volts called la margarita (the daisy), which left deep ulcerations which I still have and which caused a violent contraction, as if all my limbs were being torn off at once, especially in the kidneys, legs, groin and sides of the body. They also put a wet rag on my chest to increase the intensity of the shock.

This witness's testimony, horrifying as it is in its prosaic matter-of-factness, is common enough in the annals of electrical torture. Its reference to 'intense therapy', though, is significant, pointing as it does to the electro-convulsive therapy (ECT) used for the treatment of the mentally ill. Developed in the 1930s by the Italian psychiatrists Cerletti and Bini, ECT set out to reprogramme the disturbed mind by means of skillfully administered electric shocks. They were delivered by a voltmetered apparatus through electrodes, which were typically attached to the patient's temples.

Just how direct the connection is between ECT therapy and torture is hotly disputed. Some scholars deny that there is any real connection at all, maintaining that modern electroshock torture owes far more to the electrical picana, or cattle prod, developed in the Buenos Aires stockyards of the 1930s than it does to the Italian ECT device, a small-scale affair that delivered only a lightbulb's worth of charge (yet was nonetheless painful). Nevertheless, this rationalization cannot blind us to the fact that, during the 20th century, there has been a clearly discernible tendency towards what Amnesty International's Medical Commission calls 'the growing use of medical skill in repression'. ECT, for example, became a key component in the repressive tactics of many governments and regimes. No sooner had the tide of the World War II

All fully activated and ready to go: pain arcs across the terminals of a state-of-the-art, electroshock stun-gun, as used by US law-enforcement officers as recently as 1999.

When torture began in countries such as Argentina, it often drew on the application of electroshock. During the 1970s, 30,000 people were imprisoned and many of them tortured; an annual march is held to demand an accounting for the victims.

begun to turn in the Allies' favour than the CIA's chief psychologist was recommending that, once victory had been attained, 'each surviving German over the age of 12 should receive a short course of electroshock treatment to burn out any remaining vestige of Nazism.'

ECT evolved out of a theory that reduced human psychology to its most mechanistic components and conceived of the disturbed mind as a sort of wobbly TV picture, which might be restored to coherence by a well-timed thump. The original practitioners of ECT may have had good intentions, but in hindsight the analogy between shock-therapy and torture is all too clear.

After its first major appearance in French Algeria, electrical torture arguably came of age in Latin America during the security clampdowns of the 1970s – ironically in countries that had long prided themselves on their European sophistication. Uruguay was known as 'South America's

Switzerland'; Chile saw itself as the region's England; while Argentina's self-consciously metropolitan capital, Buenos Aires, boasted a higher percentage of the population in psychoanalysis than anywhere else in the world. So when torture began in these countries, it took the electrified form it did in part because they had reputations to protect, but in part, too, because electricity seemed to sanitize brutality, and could be rationalized, perversely, as 'treatment'.

Electrical Restraints

The application of electroshock as a type of invasive psychotherapy represented something of a break with torture tradition. Soon, torturers were reverting to type, forsaking this quasi-medical model of 'treatment' in favour of one based on the herding of cattle in stockpens and abattoirs. Both the brand and the whip had originated in the same way, so it was no surprise when the electric cattle prod was likewise appropriated. Where the ECT device was cumbersome, expensive and comparatively weak in charge, the new prod technology increasingly allowed maximum power in the most portable of forms. The tool's origins in the livestock industry were obscured by its alternative and more neutral-sounding title of 'stun-gun'. The torturer's implement is not literally a 'cattle prod' but a purpose-designed weapon. Nevertheless, the two types of device are certainly closely related, and they share common, and continual, design modifications.

By the end of the 1960s, reports of police officers in the American South charging civil rights protestors with 'electric cattle prods', which were routinely deplored in the liberal United States and European media. Yet in the same decade, and routinely ever since, other 'non-lethal' devices, introduced for police and personal protection, have been almost universally acclaimed on humanitarian grounds. Although it is in general preferable to be temporarily incapacitated by a jarring shock, however painful, than to be fatally wounded, electrical weapons can be as 'lethal' as any other.

Alongside the stun-gun, the 'taser' also evolved. Using compressed air to shoot a pair of tiny darts trailing threadlike cables through which a 2–3-second charge of 50,000 volts was delivered, this weapon could deal an immobilizing jolt to any would-be skyjacker without any risk of damaging the aircraft by firing off a gun. On the streets, the taser allowed law-enforcement officers to tackle a violent suspect without having to get too close. Again, the arguments in favour of the weapon are, as far as they go, not unpersuasive. The problem lies in the weapon's potential for abuse in the hands of the unscrupulous, as chillingly demonstrated, in

Electricity seemed to sanitize brutality, and could be rationalized, perversely, as 'treatment'

1991, by the notorious attack on Rodney King by members of the Los Angeles Police Department. The taser used by police not only contributed considerably to the victim's suffering in its own right, but also made his limp body that much more vulnerable to violent blows.

The electric riot shield, which administers a shock to a violent prisoner pinned up against iron bars, is similarly defensible in its proper place and under correct conditions of use. Yet once more, controversy arises when the weapon is 'misused'. While appearing in a San Diego court on assault charges, Edward Váldez chose to wear an electric 'stun belt' instead of the usual shackles and chains, in order to make a more positive impression on the jury. Yet when his guard accidentally discharged the suspect's shock belt, Váldez screamed and collapsed on the floor in the courtroom hallway, losing consciousness for about a

An electric stun-shield is shown off in an American County Sheriff's Office: a charge of 75,000 volts can be delivered through the vertical strips at the touch of a button.

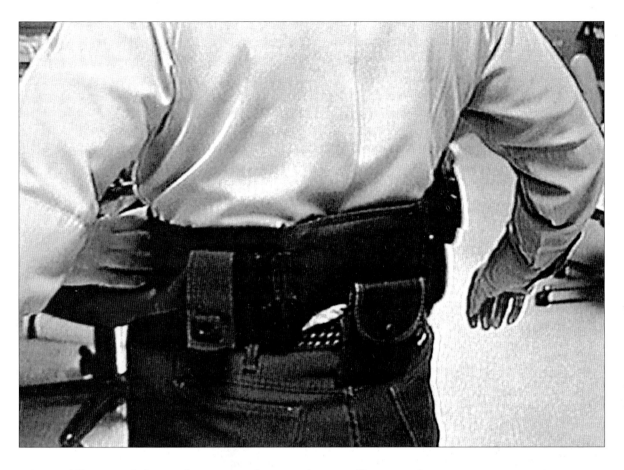

minute. The stun belt can be operated remotely at a distance of up to 91m (300ft), delivering some 50,000 volts to the left kidney, from where the shock spreads throughout the entire body via nerves and blood vessels. The prisoner is paralyzed for several minutes, and the shock is often accompanied by urination and defecation, reducing the adult to a humiliating state of incontinent babyhood. The scope for abuse with such a weapon is only too apparent.

As with all such 'electrical restraints', human rights watchdogs suspect that the devices are being designed specifically to be 'misused' by torturers worldwide on a massive scale. Indeed, at a time when torture has never been more strongly condemned by a well-informed, international public, the trade in its instruments has never been so brisk – or, for that matter, so respectable. If seemingly benign western governments aren't actively encouraging this trade, then many are certainly choosing to look the other way.

Padlocked to prevent its removal, an electric stun-belt is fitted round the waist of an official demonstrator in another scene from Amerian law-enforcement life at the start of the 21st century.

Chapter Ten

Mental Cruelty

In 1983, Darrell Cannon, a habitual criminal, was picked up by officers from the Chicago Police Department and taken for a drive. He alleges that they stopped on a patch of empty wasteground on the outskirts of the city and made him get out of the car. Cannon said that a man in his position could expect the police to 'beat you up a little bit, put a few bruises on your head', but what happened next, if true, belongs in another category of abuse entirely. In the story he told to journalist Sasha Abramsky,

> Cannon alleges that first the officers suspended him by his arms, which were handcuffed behind his back. Then, he says, an officer pulled a shotgun from the car's trunk and showed Cannon the shell in its chamber, saying 'Look at this, nigger.' According to Cannon, the officers then forced the gun into his mouth, and pulled the trigger – but through a sleight of hand, the cops had slipped the shell out of the gun's barrel. The trigger clicked, Cannon's hair stood on end, and the officers started laughing, he says: 'In my lifetime, I'd never experienced anything remotely close to this.'

The experience may have been new to Cannon, but many others have endured mock-execution – most famously the Russian writer and political prisoner Fyodor Dostoyevsky, who in 1849 was marched out to face a firing squad, which then did not fire. He was subsequently exiled to Siberia. A torture that takes its victim to the very threshold of death before laughingly slamming shut the door touches the very deepest human fear.

Manipulation of fear has always been as integral to the act of torture as the application of physical pain; hence the tradition of first allowing the prospective victim to view the executioner's equipment. Fear is used by torturers not as an end in itself, but for its capacity to break down an individual's sense of self, destroying in the process all resolve and sense of purpose. Even more significant than the natural fear of death is the psychological confusion caused by confounded anticipation. The man who has fully expected to die is not disappointed, of course, to find himself still alive, but he most certainly experiences profound disorientation. Taken to the very edge of extinction, and then suddenly snatched back from the brink, he no longer knows what to think or how to react.

An inmate of Russia's Chernokozovo detention camp eyes the outside world distrustfully through the slot in his cell door: whatever its physical cruelties, torture's most profound effects are invariably upon the mind.

Will the shots come or won't they? For two of his comrades the answer was a bitter 'yes', but this prisoner of the Mexican Civil War could either die instantly or live to be haunted for the rest of his days by his mock-execution.

The theory of fear

According to the CIA's *Human Resource Exploitation Training Manual* (obtained under the Freedom of Information Act by reporters working for the *Baltimore Sun* in 1994), the purpose of all 'coercive interrogation' is to induce 'psychological regression'. The manual explains that:

> Regression is basically a loss of autonomy, a reversion to an earlier behavioral level. As the subject regresses, his learned personality traits fall away in reverse chronological order. He begins to lose the capacity to carry out the highest creative activities, to deal with complex situations, or to cope with stressful interpersonal relationships or repeated frustrations.

He is, in short, reduced to helpless infantilism, a state in which normal values and loyalties – even his own long-term safety or well-being – will count for nothing beside the need for comfort in the immediate moment. The CIA manual, which is known to have been circulated among client governments in Central and South America and elsewhere, maps out some of the many different ways in which 'regression' can be encouraged, whether or not accompanied by the use of physical force. The 'coercive techniques' start, it is made quite clear, from the moment of arrest:

> The manner and timing of the subject's arrest should be planned to achieve surprise and the maximum amount of mental discomfort. He should therefore be arrested at a moment when he least expects it and when his mental and physical resistance is at its lowest – ideally, in the early hours of the morning. When arrested at this time, most subjects experience intense feelings of shock, insecurity, and psychological stress, and have great difficulty adjusting to the situation.

The circumstances of detention, too, have a major bearing. According to the CIA manual:

> A person's sense of identity depends upon the continuity in his surroundings, habits, appearance, relations with others, etc. Detention permits the questioner to cut through these links and throw the subject back upon his own unaided internal resources. Detention should be planned to enhance the subject's feelings of being cut off from anything known and reassuring.

The common theme of all these techniques is the disruption of every sort of certainty

'Deprivation of sensory stimuli', 'threats and fear', 'pain' and other factors may all be used, as may a number of 'noncoercive techniques', which the manual lists as follows: 'persistent manipulation of time; retarding and advancing clocks; serving meals at odd times; disrupting sleep schedules; disorientation regarding day and night; unpatterned questioning sessions; nonsensical questioning; ignoring halfhearted attempts to cooperate; rewarding noncooperation.' The common theme of all these techniques is the disruption of every sort of certainty – those assumptions, great and small, on which every one of us depends. Chip away enough at the little things – our sense that we know what time of day it is or what we are talking about in any given exchange – and our sense of individual integrity begins to fall to pieces.

Who's brainwashing who?

Although the CIA revelations may have shocked readers of the *Baltimore Sun*, these insights would have come as no surprise to any of the world's torturers, past or present. However, while all torture works on a 'psychological' level – in that it acts upon the body as a means of swaying the mind – the systematic attempt to bypass physical abuse and act directly upon a subject's psyche does seem to have originated in the 20th-century.

The sort of 'regression' the CIA's experts describe helps account for cases in which individual prisoners have confessed, without apparent duress, to crimes of which they are afterwards proved innocent. In a series of well-publicized miscarriage-of-justice cases in the Britain in the 1990s, those exonerated had almost all been convicted on the basis of confessions extracted by bullying and severe intimidation – although the methods used stopped well short of anything that would traditionally have been described as 'torture'. Because the defendants seem to have been browbeaten only for a short time, the British courts did not believe their subsequent retractions. Far more shocking, and on an altogether larger scale, were the many hundreds of Stalin's victims who ingenuously admitted to appalling offences during the show trials of the 1930s. Strangest of all, though, were the American POWs paraded in wartime Korea, who spoke in a zombie-like monotone as they espoused Communist Party jargon in acknowledging their 'crimes against the people'.

Revisionist scholars have been quick to dismiss 'brainwashing' as no more than an American myth

Revisiting the Cold War years with the benefit of hindsight and historical detachment, revisionist scholars have been quick to dismiss 'brainwashing' as no more than an American myth. Though no doubt much exaggerated in western propaganda, attempts were indeed made to systematically reorder prisoners' thought processes and memories. The idea that the mind was more mechanism than organism, and might therefore be scientifically remodelled, had considerable appeal for those in power in many parts of the world in the mid-20th century. Users of electrical torture, in particular, regarded the human brain in precisely these terms.

In recent decades, the advanced science of 'artificial intelligence' has made it clear that, even if the human brain could be regarded as a quasi-computer, it would be far too sophisticated to be readily reprogrammed. By the 1950s, however, this area of study was not even in its infancy. In the Communist countries of the time, there was on the one hand great optimism about the potential for progress through technology and, on the other, a materialistic impatience with 'bourgeois' attempts to 'mystify' the workings of the human mind and see it as something too complex and elaborate to be understood.

The sort of techniques specifically associated with brainwashing – repetitive chanting of slogans, as well as interminable sessions of commissar-led 'self-criticism' – would, when accompanied by other forms of disorientation, certainly have done much to undermine a victim's sense of psychological autonomy. Such strategies might even have had lasting results. Once damaged, the delicate human psyche does

With actual evidence for the alleged' 'genocide' in Kosovo proving elusive, NATO ministers, keen to justify the 1999 bombings, had to make do with a supposed Serbian 'torture-centre'. Pride of place here is taken by a hangman's noose, undeniably chilling in its symbolism whether or not it saw action in reality.

not easily recover. But the 'Manchurian Candidate' thesis – the belief that brainwashed captives could be fashioned into amoral communist robots programmed to undermine western society from within – was from the start nothing more than a far-fetched fantasy. Talk of 'brainwashing' and high-flown theories of 'regression' may too easily mask the fact that in practice psychological – like physical – assaults have been brutally crude more often than cleverly refined.

When used as a means of torture, rape is as much about psychological as physical violence. The case of the father forced by Chilean security agents to sodomize his own son, for instance, involves an attack on the subject's deepest and most highly cherished instincts. Other related forms of psychological duress may be subtler. Women prisoners in Northern Ireland's Armagh prison in the 1980s alleged that the strip-searches they were subjected to were, in effect, nothing less than a form of violation. They won support from international human

Blindfolded, confused and disorientated, these Vietnamese prisoners of war will start out with a crushing disadvantage when the psychological battle with their interrogators gets under way.

A North Korean captive and a South Korean intelligence officer chat politely. Propaganda certainly, but this image still embodies a genuine truth: the Korean War of 1950–53 did indeed see a shift towards subtler psychological approaches to interrogation.

rights organizations, despite the authorities' insistence that the searches were necessary to maintain a secure regime. An Amnesty International report from Shandong province, China, described how a group of young women were forced to submit to internal examinations in the presence of jeering male prison officers. Those conducting the checks were genuine doctors, and justification was claimed on medical grounds. But the effect of the women's humiliation was profoundly damaging, and there can be little doubt that this was the real object of the exercise.

Almost routinely down the ages, victims have been compelled to inflict torture on one another, at appalling cost to their own belief system and self-worth. The prisoner told that the screams from an adjacent chamber are a parent's or partner's is being subjected to a terrible form of torment – even if it subsequently emerges that the claim was false. Helplessness in the face of another's suffering can, in its way, be as bad as physical torture. The Tibetan Centre for Human Rights and Democracy received clear evidence of this in testimony from Tibetan prisoners forced by Chinese officers to watch video footage of fellow activists under torture – the distress is especially severe when the victim is a Buddhist monk, and thus a powerful symbol of national and religious identity. Symbolism matters, of course, both to torturers and their victims. As recounted in James Pettifer's *The Turkish Labyrinth: Ataturk and the New Turkey* (1997), when Turkish interrogators used

Ivan Pavlov, the founder of 'Behaviourism'. He saw the mind as a mechanism that could be manipulated by chemical and physical triggers, a useful concept in social control.

burning cigarettes to trace out the letters 'TC', for 'Republic of Turkey', on a Kurdish prisoner's skin, they not only inflicted intense pain but delivered a calculated insult to his people's separatist aspirations.

Test of sanity

'We didn't liquidate them when we had the chance. Now we must make the most of the time we have left to drive them mad.' So said Major Maciel, sometime director of Uruguay's paradoxically named Libertad (Liberty) Prison, an institution apparently geared to the systematic destabilization of its inmates' psyches. During nine years of military dictatorship, dissidents were incarcerated in Libertad, subjected to an array of disturbing tests and 'treated' with electro-convulsive therapy and psychotropic drugs. Isolation, sleep deprivation, disorientation – all the usual techniques for inducing 'regression' were applied to the prison population on a massive scale. Most fearsome of all were the effects of Libertad's many narcotic treatments. One former prisoner of Libertad, Antonio Mas Mas, recalled his experience of calmancial, a fluphenazine-based drug:

It must have been 30 minutes before I began to feel itchy all over and a lump in my throat. I had violent palpitations, my lower jaw went stiff. I sat down on the floor, I couldn't think about anything.

Similar treatments were carried out elsewhere in Latin America during the 1970s. They were used not only as a means of torture that left no obvious marks, but also to 'correct' any behaviour perceived as 'abnormal', from sexual 'deviancy' to political dissent. Such thinking seems to have underpinned the notorious programme of punitive psychiatry embarked upon by the Communist government of the Soviet Union. Like Libertad, the Soviet Union's 'Special Psychiatric Hospitals' were cynically used as a dustbin for those the government wanted out of its way. The institutions also reflected the rigid orthodoxy governing the whole discipline of soviet psychiatry, in particular the theories of Ivan Pavlov. The founder of 'Behaviourism', Pavlov's approach to human psychology stemmed from the idea that the mind was really no more than a neuro-chemical machine. Most famously, he had taught dogs to salivate at the ringing of bells, which the dogs had come to associate with the supply of food. He saw the mind as a mechanism that could be made to conform by physical and chemical triggers. The soviet psychiatric system embraced Pavlov's ideas, especially his view that mental illness was caused by chemical imbalances in the brain and central nervous system. Accordingly, psychiatrists rushed to ply their patients with a range of tranquillizers.

Programmes of aggressive 'psychotherapy' went hand in hand with courses of psychotropic drugs. The primary function of these drugs may originally have been to ensure patient cooperation for the convenience of hospital staff, but, as time went on, they were aimed specifically at inducing a range of unbearable side effects – in short, they were a form of torture. As one doctor testifies:

> The greatest intensity of inhibitory effects is regarded as the appropriate result. The sedative effect is pursued to the point of stupor. This results in more or less massive disturbances in the train of thought, a positive destructuring of the mind. On top of these direct effects there are also distressing sensations, which can be extremely painful.

The favourite drug of the soviet system was sulfazine, a suspension of elemental sulphur in peach oil. It had been used for a while in some western asylums in the 1920s and 1930s for certain categories of extreme schizophrenia, but was abruptly discontinued. Originally designed as a treatment for malaria, sulfazine is pyrogenic, inducing a violent fever in the patient, along with nausea, mental disorientation and muscle spasms. As one survivor, 'Alexei', an ex-inmate at Dnepropetrovsk Special Psychiatric Hospital, put it:

> People go into horrible convulsions and get completely disoriented. Their body temperature rises to 40 degrees centigrade almost instantly, and the pain is so intense they cannot move from their beds for three days.

'This results in more or less massive disturbances in the train of thought, a positive destructuring of the mind'

Sulfazine is simply a way to destroy a man completely. If they torture you and break your arms, there is a certain specific pain and you can somehow stand it. But sulfazine is like a drill boring into your body that gets worse and worse until it's more than you can stand …

Apart from the horrific nausea and disorientation the drug caused, the muscle spasms were so strong that sufferers could no longer use their legs or even sit down, with the result that they were forced to lie face down on their beds, effectively paralyzed. They relied on other inmates – if any were sufficiently considerate or *compos mentis* – to bring them food. In the Soviet Union's Special Psychiatric Hospitals, sulfazine was 'prescribed' in courses that went on for weeks and months, and in some cases, reportedly, even years.

However, drugs were not always required to induce disorientation and disturbance. Simply incarcerating sane prisoners alongside the insane could be almost as destructive to the well-balanced psyche. As Natalia Gorbanevskaya, a dissident who was detained for a year in a soviet Special Psychiatric Hospital, explained:

There was an everyday kind of torture which consisted of a thought, a constant image that arose from what I saw around me in the psychiatric hospital: people out of touch with their surroundings. You say to yourself: that's what I may be like tomorrow. You begin to check up on yourself every morning, looking for the first signs of madness.

All torture, arguably, has been at base psychological, its physical abuses directed ultimately at the mind. Only in the 20th century,

A day in the life of the Lubianka: Stalin's secret police set to work on the loyal commissar Kreskinski, only the latest to fall from favour, in 1938, at the height of the show trials.

though, did torturers learn to bypass the body, applying their torments directly to the suffering psyche. An advance? Some would say so, pointing to the rent flesh and broken limbs of the torture victims of ages past: those who have actually undergone psychological torture would scarcely be so sanguine.

Chapter Eleven

Capital Punishment

Flanks steaming, the horses snorted and heaved as they clattered and stumbled up the stony path. Their riders, wearied as they were by weeks of campaigning, could scarcely contain their excitement. Only a few more steps and they would see Tirgoviste, the Transylvanian capital they had come to conquer. A party of scouts for Mohammed II's mighty army, they dismounted at the top of the ridge. But even these hardened campaigners blanched as they looked down on the valley floor below, transfixed by the hellish prospect that lay before them. For miles around the city, a forest of poles reared skyward. There must have been 20,000 in all, each surmounted by a grotesque human form. Some lived still, and seemed to twitch. Gagging and choking, the Turks fell to their knees, the sudden stench of death unmanning them completely – they would never forget their entrance into the infernal world of Vlad the Impaler.

King Vlad III Tepes, 'the Impaler' – the man on whom Bram Stoker would one day base his vampire Dracula – actually existed, and all the sources concur on his savage cruelty. He is believed to have favoured a method of impaling that used horses to stretch his victim's limbs while a sharpened stake was slowly inserted into the body, sometimes into the rectum or vagina. The stake was then pushed through until it emerged out of the mouth. Alternatively, the victim was simply placed atop a sharpened pole to impale himself by the force of his own weight pushing slowly downward. Properly organized, impalement was a fearfully slow and lingering death, lasting many hours or even days. It was done slowly, to avoid shocking the victim into heart failure, and the point of the stake might be oiled to facilitate its passage through the body. Vlad clearly took pleasure in his work, and is reputed on occasion to have banqueted amid the dying, delighted by the screams and wailing coming from all around him. Creative in his own bestial, not to say demonic, way, he would order the stakes to be arranged in concentric rings or geometric patterns, or have babies skewered on the same stakes as their mothers. Most dreadful of all was the sheer scale of Vlad's excesses. Thousands of men and women were regularly impaled at a single time. Mohammed II apparently turned back in disgust when he saw the sight

The block and axe, and the executioner's mask, from the Tower of London. Though an incomparably menacing image, as methods of capital punishment go, beheading was, in fact, a merciful release.

that greeted his scouts that day in 1461 – the conqueror of Constantinople would not do battle with so hellish a monster.

The bitter cross

Impalement was employed as a punishment many centuries before Vlad would so enthusiastically make it his own. Archaeological evidence suggests that the Pharaohs of Egypt used it at least 4000 years ago. They set convicted criminals and political opponents on sharpened stakes to die slowly in the sun; and it seems probable that rulers in other ancient civilizations followed their example. Certainly, by the beginning of the Christian era (from 1 AD), impalement was practised throughout the Near and Middle East, though victims are thought to have been pinned to tree trunks with nails of bronze or iron. Eventually, this punishment would evolve into what we now know as crucifixion, in which the victim is nailed by hands and feet to a wooden cross or frame. So ubiquitous has the cross become as a Christian symbol that we tend to forget that this form of execution was used well before Christ and far beyond the 'Holy Land', from Carthage to Scythia. Crucifixion was used by Greeks and Persians as well as Romans and Jews, and was probably spread throughout the ancient world by the seafaring Phoenicians.

Though no strangers to extreme cruelty, the Romans never quite conquered their feeling that crucifixion was a barbaric punishment

The accounts of Christ's Passion given in the Gospels provide as good a description as we have of this terrible torture, though there were doubtless many minor variations on the same essential theme. Where Jesus, according to The Bible, had to carry the cross himself, most victims would have carried only the weighty transverse beam, the upright being set permanently in the ground. Reaching the execution site, the prisoner would be laid down, arms outstretched along the beam, his hands carefully fastened in position. The beam, with its prisoner attached, was then hauled up into place, either in the form of a cross or the letter 'T'. Though no strangers to extreme cruelty, the Romans never quite conquered their feeling that crucifixion was a barbaric punishment, and thus reserved it for slaves and foreigners – those not entitled to the status of citizen. Hence the particular ignominy of this execution for a 'King of the Jews'.

Death by hanging

Though Jesus was nailed to the cross, crucifixion was not primarily a punishment by impalement – indeed many victims were bound into position with lengths of cord. What killed crucified men and women was not blood loss or violent trauma, but the creeping effects of thirst, hunger, exhaustion and, finally, slow suffocation, as the unsupported

His soul rising heavenwards above his suffering body, the apostle St Andrew expires upon his X-shaped cross, as imagined by the great 15th-century French painter Jean Fouquet.

This anonymous print dating from the 16th century shows execution by hanging in its most basic form, the victim simply being 'turned off' from the rungs of a ladder, then left to dangle and slowly suffocate.

abdominal muscles buckled in on the gasping lungs. In that respect, crucifixion can be regarded as predecessor to the hangings of the modern era.

Hanging was practised in Anglo-Saxon Britain as early as the 5th century. From its inception as an official means of punishment by death, the Anglo-Saxons used purpose-built gibbet posts or wooden scaffolds. Of the technicalities, there is little to be said. Medieval representations show the victim simply being 'turned off' from a ladder leaned up against the gallows beam. They would have kicked helplessly for many minutes, even hours, slowly strangled by their own weight, unless a friend or sympathetic bystander stepped in to pull them down and put them out of their misery by breaking their necks.

This method prevailed until the 17th century, when the prisoner was instead placed standing on the back of a cart. On the executioner's signal, the horse was urged forward and the victim left to 'swing' in space. This development was more superficial than substantive – it lent an appearance of automation to what was still the old Anglo-Saxon hanging. Only in the second half of the 18th century would philanthropic campaigners, motivated by Enlightenment values, successfully agitate for the 'drop' that (in theory, at least) killed the prisoner outright. For much of early-modern history, therefore, hanging was protracted and unnecessarily cruel. Yet it would still have seemed simply a form of 'capital punishment' had it not been such a public ordeal for its victims – and had it not, so often, been bundled together with other punishments which were quite clearly means of torture.

Hung, drawn and quartered

Some confusion surrounds the precise meaning of this most infamous of punishments, a confusion that is embedded in the very wording used to describe it:

That you be carried to the place from whence you came, and from thence you shall be drawn upon a Hurdle to the Place of Execution where you shall be hanged by the Neck and, being alive, cut down; Your Privy Members shall be cut off and Bowels taken out, to be burned before your face, your Head severed from your body and your Body divided into four quarters, and they to be disposed of at the King's Pleasure. And the God of infinite mercy have mercy upon your Soul.

The Gunpowder Plot conspirators – Robert Catesby, Thomas Percy and Guy Fawkes – endure the insults and missiles of the mob, as they are drawn through the streets of London on lengths of fencing.

Though the 'drawing' of a prisoner on a hurdle (a length of fencing) through the streets before cheering, jeering crowds was an essential part of the punishment, the word 'drawing' actually seems to have referred to the 'drawing' out of his living entrails. Brought to the very brink of death by hanging, the prisoner would be cut down and laid upon a

table, his belly slit open and his viscera pulled out before his eyes. If he were in the hands of a truly skilful executioner, he would still be alive as his guts were burned in an adjacent fire and the beating heart was carefully extracted from his traumatized body. Only then would he be allowed to die, as his head was cut off and the quartering of his body began. His carcass was cut into hunks of human meat for display at different points around the kingdom. Parboiled first, so it might last longer in the open air, the human meat was set on spikes in public places as a warning to anyone else who might be tempted into the ways of treason.

William Wallace, the Scottish patriot, met his death this way in 1305. His head was displayed on London Bridge, while his four quarters were hung on gibbets far to the north at Newcastle, Berwick, Perth and

'Justice must be seen to be done': a huge crowd turns out for the public execution of a black man found guilty of the robbery and murder of a 70-year-old woman at Owen's Borrow, Kentucky, in 1936.

Stirling. According to Edward I, a man who committed treason against the Crown wronged not only his king, but also God and his fellow subjects. This is supposed to have been the logic behind the threefold death implied by this punishment: death by strangulation, death by disembowellment and death by decapitation. Apart from the appalling physical sufferings involved in such a fate, the sentence would have spread terror, too, because of the belief that dissection and dispersal robbed the soul of the body it would need afterwards as it faced eternity.

Public spectacle

The early 18th century in England witnessed hanging on an unprecedented scale, with this very public form of execution taking centre-stage in the nation's ritual and recreational life. By 1765, no fewer than 165 offences were punishable by hanging, a figure that had risen to over 200 by the start of the 19th century. The list of capital offences included: shoplifting an item worth over five shillings; wearing a disguise whilst committing a crime; poaching or vandalism in the royal forests; and, famously, stealing a sheep or other item of livestock. One inevitable consequence of this 'Bloody Code', as it was universally known, was the reluctance of juries to convict, or judges to pass the utmost sentence. Pardons were commonplace, and the Crown employed the system as a means of publicizing its mercy and compassion. However, a steady stream of public executions was always maintained since the Crown also wished to demonstrate its authority.

Public executions were observed by the general populace as a semi-official holiday, with businesses closing up for the day and crowds taking to the streets in their thousands. The procession of the prisoner from Newgate Gaol to the gallows at Tyburn, near modern-day Marble Arch – in theory a solemn warning – soon acquired the atmosphere of a carnival. Far from gravely contemplating the crimes of the convicted, the mob cheered them as heroes and frequently plied them with drinks as they passed. Even the condemned often seemed to partake in the merrymaking. Novelist Samuel Richardson was 'much disappointed at the unconcern and carelessness' he saw in certain prisoners on their way to execution, and while a certain poetic licence is doubtless at work in Jonathan Swift's story of Tom Clinch, the anecdote is entirely in keeping with the raucous festivity that had come to characterize the 'hanging fair':

> As clever Tom Clinch, while the Rabble was bawling,
> Rode stately through Holbourn to die in his Calling;

Public executions were observed by the general populace as a semi-official holiday

Brought to the brink of death by hanging, a German prisoner is laid out on the ground to receive his coup de grâce, *apparently not on but underneath the dreaded wheel.*

He stopt at the George for a Bottle of Sack.
And promis'd to pay for it when he'd come back.

Rather less robust in his attitudes than Swift, the scabrous satirist, Richardson was horrified by what he saw around Tyburn Tree itself:

At the place of execution, the scene grew still more shocking; and the clergyman who attended was more the subject of ridicule than of their serious attention. The psalm was sung amidst the curses and quarrelling of hundreds of the most abandon'd and profligate of mankind: upon whom (so stupid are they to any sense of decency) all the preparation of the unhappy wretches seems to serve only for the subject of a barbarous kind of mirth, altogether inconsistent with humanity.

As pointed out by Henry Fielding, another novelist of the period (as well as a magistrate), such debauchery made a mockery of any claim that might be made for execution's deterrent value. Time was running out for such spectacles, however. Although the Bloody Code would only get bloodier as the 18th century wore on, there were radical changes in its administration. Tyburn Tree was felled, and the hangings moved to a scaffold outside the doors of Newgate Prison. Executions were still held in public, but without the procession and its attendant revelry. The increased use of the drop also helped to reduce the visual appeal of the execution, though it was unreliable enough for execution-goers to anticipate witnessing a 'dance of death'. Not until 1868 would the last public hangings take place in both England and Scotland, but by then the authorities were already restricting the people's view as far as possible. The show was over.

Breaking on the wheel

If Britain's Bloody Code seemed brutal, convicts across the Channel fared even worse if punished by 'breaking on the wheel'. A torment originating in medieval Europe, it underwent something of a renaissance in 18th-century France and Germany. As with hanging in Britain, it was very much a public torture. Whether a real cartwheel was used, or

As recorded by a French artist in 1901, a public execution Spanish style: two murderers are garrotted back to back before a watching crowd.

simply a couple of beams crossed over one another to make an 'X', the technique involved was all too simple. The victim was tied down, spread-eagled on his back upon the rough-and-ready frame. The executioner then took an iron bar or sledgehammer and smashed each of the victim's limbs once or twice in turn. If he were lucky, these would be immediately followed by a final, fatal stroke to the stomach or chest. Timing was largely left to the discretion of the executioner, though, and sometimes a judge would expressly forbid a prompt coup de grâce. A French justice in 1761 ruled that John Calas of Toulouse, having been accused of murdering his own son, should not be dealt his death-blow till a full two hours after his first breaking.

Strongly as it would become associated with revolutionary France, the guillotine was really just the latest model of an older device, versions of which had been used throughout Europe since medieval times. The example pictured here is from Halifax, Yorkshire.

A humane death

Since the 18th century, most nations have moved away from such savage public death ceremonies – modern instruments of capital punishment have served only incidentally as instruments of torture. Yet the reluctance of many countries to renounce the death penalty, coupled with the capacity of human executioners to err, has still meant many thousands dying in agony. The 'drop', for example, was incorporated

into the hanging process to replace slow strangulation by a quick, clean kill – the fall was supposed to snap the neck between the third and fourth vertebrae. Precise calculations of weight were made to ensure the correct result, but even a slight error could leave the victim dangling, or rip the head completely from the falling body. The old-fashioned garrotte, as employed in Franco's Spain, seemed less surgically neat, yet it was less prolonged for the victim than a botched hanging.

It is easy to forget that the guillotine was first introduced as a humanitarian measure during the French Revolution. It was certainly a vast improvement on the technique of breaking on the wheel, yet this contraption was a clear descendant of the late-medieval Scottish 'Maiden', itself derived from Italian and German models. These devices were all mechanized versions of the headman's axe, albeit in theory less prone to go wrong through human error. But Monsieur Guillotine does deserve credit for designing the guillotine's distinctive triangular blade – far more effective than the straight edges of its predecessors. Though further modified as the decades went by, the guillotine was still in public use in Paris as late as 1939.

This French revolution in execution technology has, on the whole, performed better than its more recent successors, none of which has really lived up to expectations. Developed in 20th-century America, the electric chair was envisaged as a clean and clinical means of administering death. In fact, the first shock has often failed to kill, and victims have frequently been left painfully stranded halfway between life and death for minutes at a time before their predicament has been discovered and the switch re-thrown.

The gas chamber, too, has failed to prove as 'humane' as expected. Even cyanide may not be as immediate in its effects as originally thought. When the quantities used are not correctly calculated, the victim can die in terrible pain, clinging desperately to failing life. Another 'perfect' method of execution that tends to founder on the fallibility of human executioners is the lethal injection used in many US states. A cocktail of barbiturate sodium thiopental, which 'knocks out' the victim, along with pauvalon to reduce muscle movement to the point at which breathing stops, is completed by a dose of potassium chloride, which stops the heart. Nothing could be more painless, it would seem – except that victims may have violent reactions to the drugs, or there might simply be problems establishing or maintaining IV injection. A process that is supposed to put the 'patient' under in seconds has, in reality, often taken 40–50 minutes. It has sometimes taken as long as an hour to find a suitable vein and get the drip going.

Victims have frequently been left stranded halfway between life and death

Social control by execution

There are still societies in the world in which public executions in the old style are deemed to serve a useful function. Harry Wu, the famous Chinese pro-democracy campaigner, has described the day in 1983 when he chanced upon a public execution in Zhengzhou, capital of Henan Province. 'In a city of two million it seemed that all work and school had come to a stop,' he recalled. 'I estimated later that close to half the city's population must have left their jobs and classrooms.' Soon the streets were thronged, the crowd waiting in anticipation. Then,

A later version of Thomas Edison's electric chair, photographed at New York's Sing Sing prison in 1925.

45 flatbed trucks, one after another, rolled by … at the front of each truck bed, just behind the cab, stood a condemned man bound with heavy rope. The rope ran in an 'X' across his chest and around to his back, holding in place a tall narrow sign. On the top half of each sign was an accusation: 'Thief,' 'Murderer,' 'Rapist.' On the bottom half was the accused's name, marked through with a large red 'X.'

The procession wound its way through the city to a field on the outskirts, where the prisoners were forced to kneel beside shallow graves before they were shot – the 45 shots rang out in unison, recalled Harry Wu.

Spectacles such as this are a feature of 'old school' Communist countries like North Korea and China or of countries under Islamic law in the Middle East – but it would be a mistake to assume that the end is in sight for public executions. Both the rise of Islamic fundamentalism and attitudes in the West suggest that the world is far from becoming the humanitarian utopia envisaged by liberal idealists of the 1960s. Capital punishment, long considered unconstitutional in the United States, has in recent years returned with a vengeance as political

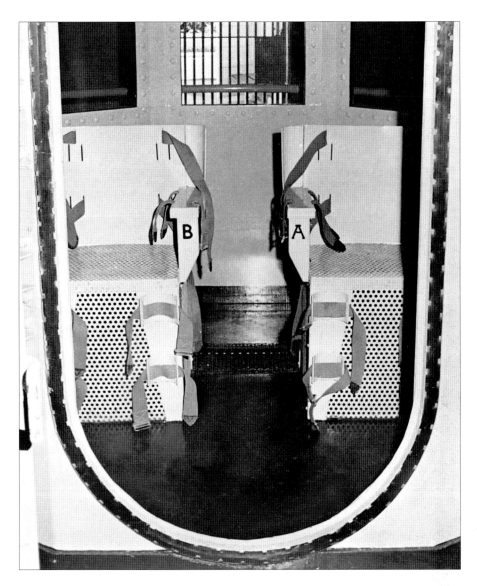

Two victims can be seated in comfort in the gas chamber at California's San Quentin prison; chair B is used for single executions since it is more accessible for the stethoscope used to monitor heartbeats.

candidates, their sensibilities finely tuned to its vote-grabbing cachet, have queued up to endorse it. And while the consumerist societies of the developed countries never explicitly approve of torture or barbarity, their moral ambivalence about inequalities and oppression in the wider world – one increasingly feeling the pressures of the global marketplace – arguably has a profound impact on the many millions for whom the instruments of torture have, most emphatically, not yet been consigned to the nightmares of history.

An End to Torture

D oubts have been expressed about the use of torture for just about as long as torture has been used, though such quiet voices as have been raised have only too readily been disregarded. The reservations of Cicero and Seneca in classical times would be picked up by St Augustine in the early centuries of the Christian church – and his concerns would strike a chord in medieval Europe in men like Peter the Chanter. Not until the days of Enlightenment, however, do we see something like a wholesale turning away from torture – and this shift in sensibility was itself arguably no more than superficial. A sceptic might argue that the consequence of this seeming revulsion was merely to displace cruel practices from their place at the heart of the justice system at home: slaves or subject nations abroad saw precious little sign of any enlightened influence in the treatment meted out to them. Even this can be seen as representing progress of a sort, yet for all the piety on display the suspicion remains that the net amount of cruelty in the world remained much the same. This trend can be said to have continued through the 20th century into our own – supposedly gentler – time. Today, in the industrialized West, when we hear reports of someone being roughed up in police custody, or of the occasional terrorist suspect being made to stand, hooded, against a wall, the ensuing media outcry points up how comparatively humane, for the most part, the system has become. That there is collective shock and outrage should, perhaps, be a source of pride; but have we really abolished torture as a norm, or merely exported it elsewhere?

Many critics would argue that the West is guilty of oppression and cruelty by proxy. Other commentators claim that western governments will back any regime on whose cooperation they think they can depend, however dismal their record on human rights and torture. Yet others have gone much further: indeed, far from being merely indifferent to such concerns, they suggest, the West actually favours repressive governments, who can be relied upon to crush democratic and trade union movements, keeping down the cost of raw material and wages on behalf of the developed countries and their multinational companies. It's a damning charge that is vigorously disputed by those who point to the achievements of western governments and firms both in driving up living standards in the Third World, and in tying aid to progress in

A vision of victory in victimhood, of transcendence in torture, Alime Mitap's drawings do not merely record the brutality of the Turkish prisons in which her own husband suffered, but suggest the strength of a human spirit that can never be completely crushed.

human rights. One thing remains certain: whether or not the West is to be held responsible for the continuation of torture in the wider world, the influence of its citizens will be essential if it is ever genuinely to be abolished. Hence the importance of non-government organizations (NGOs) in bringing pressure to bear on both politicians and business leaders – unquestionably the 20th century's most significant contribution to the campaign against cruelty worldwide.

The most famous of these organizations, Amnesty International, was founded in 1960 by London lawyer Peter Benenson. At once troubled and stirred by the news that a group of students had been arrested and imprisoned by the then fascist government of Portugal – their crime, the drinking of a public toast 'to freedom' – he launched what was originally intended to be a one-year campaign. The 'Appeal for Amnesty in 1961' was aimed at securing the release of 'prisoners of conscience' around the world. Additionally, Benenson and his fellow Amnesty activists embarked on a systematic programme of letter-writing, addressing leading statesmen on behalf of prisoners held in their countries' gaols. Not altogether surprisingly, the great world Amnesty of 1961 failed to materialize, yet at the same time it was clear that the campaign had not been entirely in vain: public attention had been drawn to the plight of prisoners and torture victims the world over. Fired by Amnesty's example, other more specialized organizations began to spring up, bringing together members of particular professions, or concentrating on abuses in specfic countries. Amnesty's campaign continued, with activists in western countries 'adopting' political prisoners, corresponding with their governments on their behalf, and contacting their families with offers of help and support whenever it was safe to do so. The human bonds thus established were one of the most important aspects of the campaign, and a key to Amnesty's appeal to newspaper readers and TV viewers in western countries, for whom human-rights issues were brought urgently to life.

Forty years on, Amnesty and other groups are still working unceasingly to investigate and support an unending catalogue of causes. It is hard to know whether to be more encouraged by their unflagging persistence or depressed by the fact that the battle is not yet won; should we celebrate the innumerable individuals whose lives have been restored to dignity, or despair that there is always another to take their place. However little headway they may appear to have made, though, the role played by these pressure groups is more vital than ever, their want of official status the very key to their success. Despite their bravura and high-sounding sentiments, our elected governors are aware that their opinions

The 'Appeal for Amnesty in 1961' was aimed at securing the release of 'prisoners of conscience' around the world

and actions are of less and less consequence in the global economy. Nowadays, the annual turnover of the biggest corporations is often greater than the gross domestic product (GDP) of many small countries, and their senior executives wield more influence than many politicians, even world leaders. This fact is often regarded, understandably, as cause for serious alarm, yet it allows for a certain, guarded optimism. Elective checks and balances may exert no influence on our new global rulers, but public opinion, and consumer purchasing power can do just that. Though apparently disenfranchised by the dwindling authority of government, today's citizens are in some ways better placed than their predecessors ever have been to influence events in the world arena.

Any reader who spends any length of time studying the history of torture is unlikely to come away with a particularly exalted view of human nature. At the same time, however, it is clear that torture, as an apparatus of state, must be considered in its political, economic, social and religious contexts. Could the comparative absence of torture in today's highly developed, industrialized nations ever conceivably be the norm throughout the entire world? Though such a prospect remains remote, and the belief in such requires enormous optimism, there is no law that says it can never be so. That it might one day be so relies, in large part, on the work of today's campaigners for human rights – ordinary men, women and children, the very people who are most often the victims of torture.

Handcuffs and thumbcuffs, as used on nationalist activists by the authorities in Chinese-occupied Tibet in the 1990s – just the latest link in a chain of torture that stretches back to antiquity.

Bibliography

Abbott, Geoff, *Rack, Rope and Red-hot Pincers: A History of Torture and its Instruments* (London, Headline, 1993)

Adams, Norman, *Scotland's Chronicles of Blood: Torture and Execution in Bygone Times* (London, Robert Hale, 1996)

Amnesty International, *Against Torture* (London, Amnesty International, 1984)

Amnesty International French Medical Commission and Marange, Valérie, *Doctors and Torture: Resistance or Collaboration?* (London, Bellew, 1991)

Bennassar, Bartolommé, *Valladolid en el Siglo de Oro* (Valladolid, Fundación Municipal de Cultura, Ayuntamiento de Valladolid, 1993)

Burford, E.J. and Shulman, Sandra, *Of Bridles and Burnings: The Punishment of Women* (London, Robert Hale, 1992)

Du Bois, Page, *Torture and Truth* (New York, Routledge, 1991)

Egido, Teófanes, *La Inquisición (Autos de fe)* (Valladolid, Obra Cultural de la Caja de Ahorros Popular, 1986)

Forrest, Duncan (ed.), *A Glimpse of Hell: Reports on Torture Worldwide* (London, Cassell/Amnesty International, 1996)

Henderson, Ernest F., *Select Historical Documents of the Middle Ages* (London, George Bell and Sons, 1910)

Hongda Harry Wu, *Laogai: The Chinese Gulag* (Boulder, CO, Westview Press, 1992)

Kamen, Henry, *The Spanish Inquisition* (Newhaven, CT, Yale University Press, 1997)

McLynn, Frank, *Crime & Punishment in Eighteenth-Century England* (London, Routledge, 1989)

Menéndez Pelayo, Marcelino, *Historia de los Heterodoxoxos Españoles* (Buenos Aires, Espasa-Calpe Argentina, 1951, originally published 1870)

Oakley, Gilbert, *Orgies of Torture and Brutality: A Historical Study* (London, Walton Press, 1965)

O'Shaughnessy, Hugh, *Pinochet: The Politics of Torture* (London, Latin America Bureau, 2000)

Parenti, Christian, *Lockdown America: Police and Prisons in the Age of Crisis* (London, Verso, 1999)

Peters, Edward, *Torture* (Philadelphia, University of Pennsylvania Press, 1996)

Pettifer, James, *The Turkish Labyrinth: Ataturk and the New Turkey* (London, Penguin, 1997)

Ruthven, Malise, *Torture: The Grand Conspiracy* (London, Weidenfeld & Nicolson, 1978)

Sangrador Vibres, Matías, *Historia de Valladolid* (1851), Edición Facsímil (Valladolid, Caja de Ahorros Provincial de Valladolid, 1979)

Saunders, Kate, *Eighteen Layers of Hell: Stories from the Chinese Gulag* (London, Cassell, 1996)

Scarry, Elaine, *The Body in Pain: The Making and Unmaking of the World* (New York, Oxford University Press, 1985)

Scott, George Ryley, *A History of Torture* (London, Bracken Books, 1994)

Index

Picture credits

Jacket
Main image: AKG London
Top: (all): Mary Evans Picture
Library
Back cover: Fortean Picture
Library

AKG London
6, 11, 12, 26, 41, 42, 45, 46,
48, 62, 65, 68, 72, 80, 84, 116,
120, 135, 136, 138, 143, 175,
176, 178, 182

Amnesty International
21, 58, 148 (Morgens
Norgaard), 150 (David

Hoffman), 151, 152, 153 (Rob
Brouwer), 156 (Rob Brouwer),
157 (Rob Brouwer), 184, 187

Associated Press
154, 158, 163

Amber Books Ltd
183

Mary Evans Picture Library
2, 8, 16, 18, 22, 25, 30, 32, 35,
36, 38, 47, 50, 54, 57, 61, 64,
66, 71, 75, 79, 82, 87, 88, 91,
96, 98, 99, 100, 102, 105, 106,
108, 110, 111, 113, 115, 117,

123, 124, 127, 128, 131, 132,
141, 144, 146, 147, 166, 168,
169, 170, 173, 174, 179

Fortean Picture Library
29, 92, 118, 142, 180

Hulton Getty
53, 76, 95

TRH Pictures
15, 114, 160, 164, 165